THE DARK SIDE OF CHRISTIAN COUNSELLING

The Dark Side of
Christian
Counselling

E. S. Williams

THE WAKEMAN TRUST, LONDON
& BELMONT HOUSE PUBLISHING

Contents

1
The Foundation of the Christian Counselling Movement

THE FLAME of psychological counselling burns brightly in the Christian church. It is a new form of ministry that finds acceptance across a wide spectrum – evangelicals, Catholics, charismatics and liberals. All alike are providing counselling services for their flocks of hurting Christians. In this book we examine the ideas and assumptions that lie behind the counselling scene. Our task is to address two questions. Is counselling, as practised by the Christian counselling movement, a legitimate part of Christian ministry? Does the church benefit from integrating psychological truth and Scripture? (A further book will explore how we should biblically view and handle problems such as depression.)

The story of the Christian counselling movement starts in the USA after the Second World War, when many pastors, under pressure from the growing psychotherapy industry, began to feel that they were not properly trained to deal with the problems of daily living that were becoming increasingly common in their congregations. The rising trend in family breakdown meant that many churchgoers were encountering anxiety and depression. Pastors were urged not to meddle with psychological problems for which they had not been properly trained – Christians suffering with deep inner hurts needed counselling by a trained psychologist.

The father of Christian counselling

In the 1950s Clyde Narramore, a Christian psychologist widely regarded as the father of Christian counselling, saw the potential for a ministry that made use of psychological counselling techniques. Through a series of talks on Christian radio entitled 'Psychology for Living', he sought to overcome the natural scepticism that many Christians felt towards psychology. As a skilled communicator he made the ideas of psychology appear acceptable to the contemporary Christian mind. His book, *The Psychology of Counselling* (1960), did much to alleviate the antagonism towards psychology felt by many in the church. In this he claimed that preaching from the pulpit is not really enough to deal with the problems of daily living that confront many people. He tells the story of a pastor who was upset when a deeply spiritual man in his congregation was picked up by the police on a serious charge. After discussing the matter with a psychologist, the pastor realised that there was a great need for psychological counselling among Christian people, and confessed that if he had allowed time for individual counselling, the man 'might not have committed this crime at all'.[1] Narramore felt that while most pastors realise the importance of the pulpit ministry, some have not fully considered the significance of such a counselling ministry to deal with personal, innermost problems.[2]

Narramore therefore set up a Christian mental health foundation in 1958 to specialise in counselling and training Christian leaders.

Fuller Theological Seminary develops a school of psychology

In May 1961 an eminent psychologist, Dr John G. Finch, delivered a series of lectures at Fuller Theological Seminary in the USA. By this time the Seminary, which was founded in 1947, had moved in a distinctly liberal direction with regard to its view of Scripture, but it was still highly influential among evangelicals. Dr Finch's psychological theories were eagerly embraced, and the idea of a School of Psychology alongside the School of Theology fitted perfectly into Fuller's vision of a social gospel. The Seminary formed a committee of distinguished psychiatrists, psychologists and theologians to work with experts in the field of psychology. A physiological psychologist was appointed Dean of the School of Psychology, and in 1965 the first students started their studies. Fuller soon secured its position as a leader in the field of Christian counselling, offering a doctoral programme in clinical psychology. Christian psychologists were presented to the churches as possessing a special ability to assist people on their journeys to spiritual and emotional wholeness.

Fuller's training programme is committed to the integration (or combining) of psychology and theology in theory, research, and practice. They claim that this 'integration' incorporates the best of psychology with Christian principles, a process that has had a major impact on the development of Christian counselling in the USA and also in the wider world.

Key figures of early days

Another significant development in the late 1960s was the founding of the Rosemead School of Psychology by Clyde and Bruce Narramore (Clyde's nephew). The purpose was to train clinical psychologists from a Christian perspective, also with a primary focus on the integration of psychology and theology.

The Christian counselling movement gained momentum during the 1970s and 1980s when many young evangelicals were persuaded to take up careers in psychology. Key personalities were James Dobson, Bruce Narramore, Gary Collins, Tim LaHaye and H. Norman Wright. A feature of these men was their ability to write self-help books that used psychological theories tempered with Christian ideals on issues such as parenting, self-image and personal growth. The best-selling books on the shelves of Christian bookstores became those that provided advice on how to live a successful life, how to deal with inner pain and how to overcome depression.

In the 1970s Dr Larry Crabb, a prominent Christian psychologist, published two books, *The Basic Principles of Biblical Counselling* (1975) and *Effective Biblical Counselling* (1977) that sought to provide a theoretical justification for Christian psychological counselling. The writing of Larry Crabb, who has published over 20 books, has had a major impact on the Christian counselling movement in the USA (Dr Crabb's model of counselling being dealt with in chapter 11).

Such was the attraction of the psychological way, that many evangelical pastors found themselves drawn to the new teaching. Pastor Steven Cole, who graduated from Dallas Theological Seminary with a Master's Degree, writes of his experience as a young pastor in the early 1980s. 'Like most of my evangelical pastor comrades, my preaching was often flavoured by the latest insights of psychology. Of course, I would never use psychological insights unless they were in line with Scripture. But, at the same time, I had been taught in seminary, "All truth is God's truth". If a psychologist stumbles across some biblical principle, why not use it? Doesn't the Bible teach proper self-love, as long as I'm not proud? Isn't God's love for me the basis for proper self-esteem? Aren't parents supposed to build their children's self-esteem? So I preached sermons such as "Feeling Good About Yourself" and "Developing a Sense of Self-Worth", based on Scripture (so I thought), laced with insights, quotes, and stories from the leading Christian psychologists, whose books and articles I read. I attended conferences where these men provided training in various aspects of pastoral ministry, counselling and communication. I used videos by Christian psychologists to help train people in things like child-rearing and marital relationships.'[3]

Pastor Cole, however, describes how he was cured of his fascination with the psychological way when he read Calvin's *Institutes of the Christian Religion*. 'As I read Calvin's solid biblical treatment of the nature of man and sin, I realised that I had erred greatly by falling into the proper self-esteem teaching of Christian psychology. I realised that Christian psychology served to build man up in his sin and to pull God down as our good buddy who loves us unconditionally so that we can accept ourselves. But the Bible builds God up as holy and glorious, while it strips man of his pride and self-righteousness . . .'[4]

Jay Adams and nouthetic counselling

In 1970 Dr Jay E. Adams, a Reformed Presbyterian theologian with a post-doctoral fellowship in psychology, challenged the integrationist view of Christian counselling with the publication of his book *Competent to Counsel* (1970). He was deeply critical of psychotherapy and insisted that all counselling should be based on the Bible rather than the godless theories of psychology. He argued that Freud had played a leading part in the collapse of responsibility in modern society. He said that Freud 'has sanctioned irresponsible behaviour and made it respectable'.[5]

Adams was also critical of the non-directive, client-centred psychotherapy of Carl Rogers, for it confirms sinful man's belief that he is autonomous and has no need of God. He said that evangelical Christians 'must reject Rogerian counselling on the basis of its humanistic presuppositions alone'.[6] He was astonished that evangelical pastors could blatantly deny their theological training in the counselling room.

Adams developed a version of Christian counselling that aimed to use Scripture to address the problems of daily living rather than the techniques of psychology. He called this approach nouthetic counselling – the term comes from the Greek noun *nouthesia*, which is translated 'to admonish, correct or instruct'. Nouthetic counselling advocates three main steps – to confront, to have concern, and to lead to change. Adams has since written a number of books with the aim of developing what he called truly biblical counselling, including *The Christian Counsellor's Manual* (1973), *The Christian Counsellor's Casebook* (1974), *A Theology of Christian Counselling* (1986), and many other books. In 1968 he co-founded the Christian Counselling and Educational Foundation (CCEF) with the aim of developing a biblical model of counselling. However, as Adams' influence declined during the 1970s the CCEF has become increasingly psychological in its orientation.

The growth of Christian counselling

Adams' critique of psychotherapy was not altogether popular, and slowly but surely Christian psychology was becoming a dominant feature of evangelical Christianity. An article in the high-circulation American magazine *Christianity Today* confidently declared:

'*Myth*: A pastor is competent to counsel his parishioners. *Fact*: Most pastors are armed with only a meagre knowledge of behavioural therapies. A pastor's calling is, primarily, a spiritual one, helping people to find strength in God's presence and a sense of divine direction in the midst of difficulty. Psychological adjustment is a different matter, and when it requires serious attention, pastors should find ways of partnering with professional counsellors or psychiatrists.'[7]

The movement to bolster biblical counsels with secular psychology continued to gain ground with the publication of *The Integration of Psychology and Theology* (1979), by John Carter and Bruce Narramore, which argued that increasingly society was looking to psychology to shed new light on the problems of human existence. They wrote that Christianity was in the throes of an encounter with psychology. 'On both academic and popular levels alike, psychology is making inroads into areas traditionally considered the domain of Christianity. And the signs of this encounter are everywhere about us. Religious bookstores are filled with volumes on psychology. A Christian periodical is incomplete without an article on some aspect of personal or family adjustment. And nearly every theological seminary offers courses in areas such as counselling, psychology and mental health. Psychologists are lecturing at Bible conferences.'[8]

The American Association of Christian Counsellors (AACC), established around 1990, believes that the helping ministry of the church must be supported by three legs – the pastor, the lay helper and the clinical professional. The vision of the Association, which now claims to have 50,000 members, is to serve the worldwide Christian church by helping to educate and equip a large army of professional clinicians, pastoral counsellors and lay helpers in the skill of counselling. It sees counselling as a case-based form of Christian discipleship that assists the church in its call to bring believers to maturity in the lifelong process of sanctification and growing to maturity in Christ.

Larry Crabb, Spiritual Director to the Association, gave the following (unrealistic) endorsement: 'The tide is turning – Christian counselling is becoming more Christ-centred, biblically-based and oriented toward the eternal more than the immediate. AACC is leading the way to be there for you.' The Vice President of Focus on the Family, H. B. London Jr, also provided his unqualified endorsement of the Association: 'We are finding that a high percentage of pastors we meet feel ill-prepared to deal with the complex pastoral counselling issues that come their way. AACC is on the cutting-edge as they seek to equip the "called out" minister for the 21st century reality.'[9]

The Christian counselling movement in the UK has absorbed many ideas from the USA. Selwyn Hughes, who many regard as the spiritual leader of Christian counselling in the UK, attended a course at Rosemead Graduate School of Psychology in the 1970s. In his auto-biography, Hughes tells how he greatly valued his time at Rosemead where he drank in every word that he was taught by Clyde Narramore. But it was Larry Crabb who had the greatest influence on his life and view of Christian counselling. We shall hear more in chapter 2 about how Hughes used his organisation – the Crusade for World Revival (CWR) – to promote Christian counselling.

Opposition to Christian counselling

In the 1980s, Martin and Deidre Bobgan expressed concern about the growing influence of psychology in the church in a series of books, that included *The Psychological Way/The Spiritual Way* (1979), *Psychoheresy: The Psychological Seduction of Christianity* (1987) and *Prophets of Psychoheresy* I (1989). The Bobgans argued that psychotherapy was creeping into the church and finding a stronghold in the minds of many. They called on Christians to reject the psychological opinions of men, and to believe in the sufficiency of the Word of God.

The Bobgans set up Psychoheresy Awareness Ministries, issuing a regular newsletter to inform Christians about psychoheresy, which they define as 'the integration of secular psychological counselling theories and therapies with the Bible'. They add, 'Psychoheresy is also the intrusion of such theories into the preaching and practice of Christianity, especially when they contradict or compromise biblical Christianity in terms of the nature of man, how he is to live, and how he changes.'[10]

Others who drew attention to problems within the Christian counsel-ling movement include Dr Richard Ganz in *PsychoBabble – the Failure of Modern Psychology and the Biblical Alternative* (1993).

A therapeutic gospel

Despite these warnings, the 1990s saw a sustained growth in the influence of the Christian counselling movement. Following the psycho-logical way, Rick Warren in *The Purpose Driven Church* (1995) claims, 'Whenever Jesus encountered a person he'd begin with their hurts, needs, and interests.'[11] In the chapter entitled 'How Jesus Attracted Crowds' he states: 'The most likely place to start is with the person's felt needs ... this was the approach Jesus used ... A good salesman knows you always start with the customer's needs, not the product.'[12]

One of the fruits of the Christian counselling scene is the emergence, over the last three decades, of a new therapeutic 'gospel' that aims to meet the psychological needs of the congregation. Such is the impact of the 'psychologising' of the Gospel that the message from the pulpit of many Bible-believing churches has undergone a subtle change, there being a growing consensus that traditional teachings about sin, wrath and judgement make the Gospel message appear unattractive in a modern world. In *Today's Gospel – authentic or synthetic?* Walter Chantry describes the message of the modern evangelist. 'Audiences are reminded that they are sad, lonely, discouraged, and unsuccessful. Life is a great weight to them. Troubles encompass them. The future holds dark threats. Then sinners are invited to come to Christ, who will change all of that and put a smile on their faces. He is pictured as a cosmic psychologist who will patch up all problems in one session on the inquiry-room couch. There is no reminder of the discipline which Christ demands. No suggestion is given that following Jesus is sacrificial and painful.'[13]

Contemporary worship has also become a vehicle for expressing the truths of the psychological way. The modern songs that have replaced traditional, doctrinally sound hymns in the majority of evangelical churches, have a strong focus on me, my emotional needs and longings. In *Losing our Virtue* David Wells draws attention to the therapeutic nature of modern songs. God is valued 'to the extent that he is able to bathe these wounds, assuage these insecurities, calm these fears, restore some sense of internal order, and bring some sense of wholeness.'[14]

Such is the commitment to the psychological way that many churches organise road-shows to help their congregation deal with the problems of daily living. Seminars on parenting refer to the latest psychological theories on disciplining children. Marriage courses help partners discover what makes them feel loved. 'They have the time to discuss ways they have caused each other pain and discover how to heal hurt.'[15] They also learn new skills for communication and conflict resolution.

The local Christian bookshop is well stocked with books that show Christians how to overcome their feelings of depression, stress, inner pain, low self-esteem and general misery. Books that offer guidance on the secrets of successful living are bestsellers. The Wesley Owen website, the largest organisation selling Christian books in the UK, lists over 200 titles that deal with Christian psychology and counselling.

The plan of this book is to explore the teaching of the Christian counselling movement. We need to examine the theological justification for integrating Scripture and psychology. We need to understand the roots from which it has emerged and this will involve a discussion of the theories of secular psychology, and the influence of men like Sigmund Freud, Carl Rogers and Abraham Maslow. We need to understand the ideas and concepts which lie at the heart of Christian counselling, such as self-esteem. We shall then be in a position to assess whether Christian counselling is a legitimate part of Christian ministry or whether it is an impostor that is misleading the church.

2
Christian Counselling in the UK

W HILE THE IDEAS that gave rise to the Christian counselling movement came largely from the USA, they rapidly
spread across the Atlantic. A loss of doctrinal certainty
around the fundamental truths of the Christian faith, a decline in expository preaching, the rise of contemporary worship, a growing interest
in innovative techniques for church growth and the emphasis on signs
and wonders had produced a worldly mindset among Christians in
the UK that was open to all new ideas. Many churches were open to
a ministry that helped hurting Christians and the teachings of Larry
Crabb, James Dobson and others proved to be irresistible.

Crusade for World Revival promotes Christian counselling

The Crusade for World Revival (CWR) has been a pioneer of
Christian counselling in the UK. In 1965 the Rev Selwyn Hughes, a
charismatic pastor, decided to set up an organisation with the aim of
inspiring a Holy Spirit revival, starting in London and spreading worldwide. Hughes explained that he was a crusader at heart who wanted
to use his voice 'in calling the church to pray for and believe God for

a flood of his Holy Spirit to flow through the worldwide church. The only word I could think of to describe that was revival. Thus the name of the charity should be Crusade for World Revival.'[1]

By the early 1970s, the revival not having taken off, Hughes was holding self-help 'Life in a New Dimension' seminars around the UK. He explains, 'Before this the emphasis had been on evangelism and revival, but now there was a strong thrust towards teaching and the equipping of Christians to handle life's problems and difficulties through the application of biblical principles.'[2] He teamed up with Trevor Partridge who had been trained in psychology at Seattle Bible College.

When CWR had been in existence for 10 years, Hughes decided to focus on its future. What lay ahead was a move into psychological counselling. While CWR's counselling seminars were well subscribed, Hughes realised that to become a leader in the field of Christian counselling he needed some training, and so he enrolled for a counselling course at the Rosemead Graduate School of Psychology in the USA. While at Rosemead he heard about Larry Crabb, an up-and-coming psychologist known for his strong stand on Scripture.

Hughes read and studied Crabb, for he saw him as the future intellectual power of the counselling movement. He found Crabb's books superb. 'My heart resonated with everything he was saying. The more I read the more I wanted to meet this man.' Hughes' wish was granted when he attended a week-long course at the Institute in Biblical Counselling in the USA. As he listened to Crabb he kept saying to himself, 'This is what I have been looking for all my life!'[3] Hughes' encounter with Crabb had transformed his thinking. He says that he felt like someone had given him a million dollars. He had learned priceless ideas which he could use to reconstruct CWR's counselling courses to make them even more effective in helping people with their problems. By incorporating Crabb's ideas, Hughes was convinced that CWR could make an even bigger contribution in the area of biblical counselling in the UK. At last Hughes had found his true calling – not world revival but psychological counselling.

Over the years the two leaders of the Christian counselling movement developed such a close bond that Crabb wrote the foreword to *Christ Empowered Living* (2001), the book in which Hughes describes his model of counselling. Crabb wrote in praise of his long-time friend.

'One thing I know. The field of counselling needs a wise voice to speak into our confusion, to lift us out of our narcissism and to direct us toward an encounter with Christ that has the power to actually change lives. Selwyn speaks with that voice.'[4]

Since the early 1990s, CWR has been running courses to train Christians in the theory and practice of counselling. According to CWR, 'Our exciting range of courses provides training for those with a heart to help others at every level. The distinctive feature of our courses is that they are all based on a firm biblical foundation, integrating biblical understanding of the human personality with the best contemporary models of counselling.'[5] Here it is important to note that the CWR model, like most Christian counselling in the UK, is integrationist in its approach, mixing ideas from secular psychology with biblical teaching. This is an important point to which we shall return in chapter 4. An intriguing question is this. How is it that an organisation set up to promote world revival has become the leading promoter of Christian counselling in the UK?

CWR has developed its counselling ministry to such an extent that it now produces world-distributed resources and training, ranging from video programmes and short courses, to comprehensive, professionally recognised programmes including a BA (Hons) in Theology and Counselling in partnership with the London School of Theology. (CWR also uses its pastoral counselling sessions to teach the latest ideas from the doctrinally errant 'emerging church' movement.)

London School of Theology

The London School of Theology, which is an interdenominational, evangelical theological college, offering undergraduate and postgraduate degrees in Theology and Counselling, acknowledges the influence of CWR in its counselling programme. 'CWR was founded by Selwyn Hughes in 1965 and has been hugely influential through its literature, seminars, and training programmes, especially in the field of counselling. Our partnership with CWR, which began in 1998, has resulted in a counselling training unique in the UK, which draws on the best that secular models can provide, integrates it with biblical and theological principles, and builds out of that integration a counselling practice which is both professionally recognised, and faithful to biblical and Christian principles.'[6]

The London School of Theology explains that Christians often feel helpless in the face of the emotional hurts that people endure. 'How can we bring hope into lives blighted by addiction, anxiety, abuse? Our Theology and Counselling course, designed to train Christian counsellors to the highest professional standards, will equip you with the understanding and skills to do this.'[7] It is an integrated approach.

The Association of Christian Counselling (ACC)

The establishment of the Association of Christian Counselling in 1992 helped to give counselling credibility in the eyes of many churches. Following discussions with representatives from a number of Christian counselling organisations across the UK, it was agreed to set up an umbrella organisation which could provide nationwide standards and a system for the accreditation of counsellors broadly acceptable to churches and other organisations. ACC defined counselling as 'that activity which seeks to help people towards constructive change and growth in any or every aspect of their lives through a caring relationship and within agreed relational boundaries, carried out by a counsellor who has a Christian worldview, values and assumptions'.[8]

ACC recognises that among Christians there is a great variety of approaches to counselling, and has produced ethics and practice guidelines. The ACC has a list of 29 UK organisations that provide training courses for those wishing to learn the skills of counselling.

Examples of Christian counselling services

(i) Spurgeon's College

Since the 1990s Spurgeon's College has been training students in the skill of counselling. Spurgeon's courses are written by the Central School for Counselling Training (CSCT) and validated by the Counselling and Psychotherapy Central Awarding Body, both of which are secular organisations. The college explains that these courses are recognised as components towards meeting the criteria for professional accreditation with the British Association for Counselling and Psychotherapy (BACP). 'Whilst the content of CSCT courses is not exclusively faith-based, they are delivered at Spurgeon's College by Christians providing a unique opportunity to study professionally recognised secular courses in a Christian environment. Students often find this a stimulating and rewarding experience.'[9] The statement that the content of the training course is not exclusively faith-based is somewhat disingenuous, for CSCT is a secular organisation that aims to provide training courses that reflect the thinking of the secular counselling profession.

Spurgeon's College believes that it is important to train students in the skills of secular counselling so that they can obtain certificates that are accredited by the British Association for Counselling and Psychotherapy. In other words, Spurgeon's has become a training centre for psychotherapists.

(ii) The Evangelical Alliance

The Evangelical Alliance, in collaboration with CWR, commissioned a survey of churches that was carried out by the Centre for Ministry Studies at the University of Wales. The research was conducted using a comprehensive questionnaire distributed to 2,570 leaders of Alliance-affiliated churches. The results of the survey, based on 754 replies, were released in September 2000. Despite the low response rate the researchers claimed that 53 per cent of clergy and other church leaders have considered leaving the ministry at some point because the pressure is so great, and 38 per cent feel overwhelmed by the complexity of pastoral care demands they face. Stress was identified by two-thirds of clergy as the most common pastoral issue, followed by marriage guidance, bereavement, loneliness and depression.

So who ministers to the ministers? The answer, in the mind of the Evangelical Alliance, is the Christian counsellor. The findings of this survey were used as a justification for setting up the Care for Pastors Network with the purpose of offering the clergy and other Christian leaders health checks, discounted holidays, retreats, training and counselling. The Alliance's deep commitment to the Christian counselling movement is clear from its website, which provides links to a number of organisations, such as CWR, the Institute of Counselling, the Oxford Christian Institute for Counselling, the Walking Wounded website and Cornerstone, a London-based professional counselling and psychotherapy service with particular expertise and understanding of clergy and Christians in lay ministry, to mention a few of the more well known.

(iii) Churches' Ministerial Counselling Service

Psychological counselling is believed to be of such value by Free Church denominations that a network of professional counsellors is sponsored by the Baptist Union, the Methodist Church, the Salvation Army, the United Reformed Church and the Free Churches' Group (acting on behalf of other Free Church denominations) to provide services for ministers and their families. The service is run by the Baptist Union and provides suitably qualified professional counsellors who can be accessed anonymously.

The Churches' Ministerial Counselling Service (CMCS) website explains: 'Ministry can bring its own stresses, and ministers are not exempt from other problems of everyday life, arising from family or personal circumstances. It is not always appropriate to seek support from a colleague or a senior person in the denomination or organisation, so the CMCS has been set up to provide confidential access to independent help.' What does it cost? Counsellors have professional fees, and these are often beyond the means of ministers, so each denomination and organisation has agreed to make up the difference between what the client can afford and the full fee.

To be employed by the CMCS a counsellor needs to be trained to diploma level and accredited with a counselling/psychotherapy organisation. In addition, the counsellor must be willing to respect the Christian context from which the clients come and their particular denominational tradition, but does not need to be a Christian.[10]

Faith in psychotherapy is such that ministers of the Gospel are assured that the service of CMCS is trustworthy because the counsellors are recognised by the British Association of Counselling and Psychotherapy (BACP). It is amazing that Christian ministers have placed their trust in the BACP, and even more amazing that they feel the need for non-directive psychotherapy to deal with their problems. Is the God of all comfort, who comforted the apostle Paul in all his tribulations, unable to comfort the troubled ministers of today? (2 Corinthians 1.3-4.)

(iv) All Souls, Langham Place

An example of Anglican acceptance of the amalgamating of secular psychology with Christian counselling is to be seen at All Souls Church,

Langham Place, which has developed a counselling service for hurting and depressed Christians. The initial service was provided by a psychologist who was involved in the teaching programme of CWR. In July 2007 Helen Willcox joined the staff of All Souls as Associate Minister for Pastoral Counselling. Her experience at St Helen's, Bishopsgate had taught her that Christians faced difficult issues. 'I realised how complicated some of the issues were that Christians faced and how limited the resources were for helping them.' This insight led her to train as a counsellor, completing a secular training course at Spurgeon's College. 'I am looking forward to using this training within the context of All Souls and helping individuals be more of the people God means them to be despite some of the damaging experiences that people face.'[11] Many other mainstream evangelical Anglican churches have become enthusiastic partners in the growing UK Christian counselling movement.

A challenge to the Christian counselling industry

The Christian counselling movement has swept like a tidal wave across the USA, and a decade later, across the UK. It is now a highly organised industry and there is hardly a church in the country that has not been touched in some way. Most branches of the Christian faith, including charismatics, evangelicals and Anglicans, have eagerly embraced all that the movement has to offer. Some churches have their own counselling service, some have trained counsellors, some have counselling seminars for their congregation, most have self-help books on their bookstall, and most churches refer members with emotional problems for counselling. Such is the acceptance of the Christian counselling ministry that the New Word Alive conference in 2008 held seminars on self-esteem, depression and bereavement counselling run by Helen Willcox from the counselling ministry of All Souls, Langham Place.

Remarkably, there has been little British published opposition to the Christian counselling industry in the UK led by CWR, the London School of Theology, the Evangelical Alliance, Spurgeon's College, the Anglican Association of Advisers in Pastoral Care and Counselling, the Churches' Ministerial Counselling Service and All Souls, Langham Place. There are, however, many 'unpublished' pastors and churches that oppose the underlying ideology of this movement.

In July 2008 an article appeared in *Evangelicals Now* challenging the credentials of the Christian depression industry. Nancy Lambrechts asked why the church sends 'God's people to professionals to pay money to talk about their suffering, their pain or their guilt? The cognitive therapist is not equipped to help, encourage, rebuke or correct the people of God, or to truly comfort them in their suffering. Why have we let the medical professionals replace the role of the church community? Because we have medicalised human suffering and sin and think the answer is primarily medical and not spiritual. How do evangelical leaders help those suffering and struggling to cope with the trials of life?' Nancy Lambrechts asks, 'Have we been deceived and led astray by a myth created by the depression industry for their own commercial gain and credibility? Have we simply accepted the deception, not discerning what is best and true?'[12]

This article was like an arrow directed into the heart of the UK Christian counselling movement. A furious response persuaded the editor to withdraw the article from the online version of *Evangelicals Now* on the pretext that some depressed people might stop their antidepressants and commit suicide. (The issue of depression will be discussed in a companion book.)

3
The Aims of Christian Counselling

W HAT IS THE PURPOSE of Christian counselling? What is it that the counselling movement hopes to achieve? In this chapter we examine the views of some of the biggest names in the Christian counselling movement, including Dr Kirsten Birkett, Frank Minirth and Paul Meier, David Seamands, Larry Crabb, Selwyn Hughes, Gary Collins and James Dobson, to understand their justification for a psychological counselling ministry.

Dr Kirsten Birkett

In her book *The Essence of Psychology* (1999), Dr Kirsten Birkett, a writer on Christian apologetics and lecturer at Oak Hill Theology College, claims that a person suffering from depression may well be able to grasp the truths of the Gospel intellectually, but the barrier of the mental illness stops the full enjoyment and living out of those truths. She argues that 'if our minds are not working properly – if our knowledge is not filtering through correctly to the rest of our beliefs – then our minds need treatment, regardless of how much we "know". Seeking therapy is not self-centred and self-indulgent, any more than going to hospital for a broken leg is. But we don't accuse people of self-indulgence when they seek treatment for a broken leg.'[1]

Birkett encourages Christians to see therapeutic counselling as a useful adjunct to their faith. Her approach is entirely pragmatic – just as we go to a doctor to get treatment for a broken leg, so we should go to a therapist to get treatment for our mind when we are not thinking correctly. She believes that if our minds are not working properly then it is the therapist who will help sort out our thinking.

But what does she mean by 'mental illness'? What is this condition that blocks the efficacy and sufficiency of the Word? Is it an extreme, irrational illness, or is it a form of depression or anxiety experienced by most people at some time? Dr Birkett, in common with most counsellors, means the latter. 'Normal' pressures evidently annul the efficacy of the Word.

But this pragmatic approach is not the way of Scripture. God's Word is profitable for doctrine, for reproof, for correction, for instruction in righteousness, that the man of God may be complete, thoroughly equipped for every good work *(2 Timothy 3.16-17)*. There is no word in Scripture to suggest that depression blocks the efficacy of the Word, and there is therefore no place for psychological techniques in transforming the mind of a Christian.

Frank Minirth and Paul Meier

Christian psychiatrists Frank Minirth and Paul Meier make a strong case for counselling in their book *Happiness is a Choice* (1994). They are upset that some lower middle-class people poke fun at those who seek professional counselling, and put it down to their naivety and defensiveness. 'Getting guidance from a knowledgeable Christian pastor or professional counsellor can help bring about victory over life's seemingly overwhelming stresses. To obtain and apply to one's life good-quality Christian counselling is synonymous with discipleship. God sanctifies many people (brings them toward Christ-likeness in their attitudes and behaviour) through confrontation by loving and insightful friends, pastors, counsellors – and even psychiatrists sometimes. Don't ever be ashamed to get counselling when going through life's stresses.'[2]

The Meier Clinics, one of the most trusted names in Christian counselling according to their website, claim to have been providing answers to life's problems since 1976. Their clinics 'are dedicated to providing a safe environment where men, women, and children can work through issues that are robbing them of satisfaction and enjoyment in life. Working together, lives are being restored daily. Thousands of individuals, couples, and families are now enjoying a more productive, fulfilling, and joyful life.'

How do you know whether you need counselling? According to the Meier Clinics' website, 'If you are thinking about whether counselling could be helpful to you, here are some questions to ask yourself: Do you ever feel really sad, frustrated, or lonely? Do you feel especially angry, annoyed, or out-of-control? Do you feel very anxious, worried, or guilty? Have you experienced some major problems at home, at work, at school, or in your neighbourhood? Have you noticed some changes in the way you sleep, eat, think, or feel about life? Is it hard for you to talk about your feelings with family or friends? Is your life being negatively affected by the way you are feeling? Is your personal life, your work and/or your relationships with family and friends more difficult than you think it should be?

'If you answered YES to any of these questions, then it may be a good idea for you to talk with a counsellor (also known as a therapist or mental health counsellor). People go to counselling for many reasons. Counselling can help you better understand your feelings and problems, and help you learn how to more effectively manage them in your everyday life.'[3] Here we should note that there are few people who would not answer yes to one of these all-embracing questions. The Meier Clinics, it seems, are suggesting that virtually every Christian needs counselling.

Selwyn Hughes of CWR

Selwyn Hughes explains that as 'a first-hand observer of the Christian life for more than fifty years, time and time again I have talked to many people who wondered aloud why, with Christ resident in their lives, they couldn't overcome the crippling anxieties, fears, compulsive thoughts or obsessive and compulsive behaviours that sometimes beset them.'[4] In his book, *Christ Empowered Living*, he tells us how he came to realise that the psychological truths from secular psychology had a lot to offer the Christian church. Hughes sees value in Albert Ellis' model of Rational Emotive Therapy, and was able to write: 'I have no difficulty with the ABC Theory of Behaviour, and I have often used it when counselling.'[5] Alfred Adler's goal-orientated psychology helped Hughes to understand human behaviour. 'The psychologist, Adler, made the point that the best way to understand any unit of behaviour is to ask yourself: What is the goal to which the behaviour is directed?'[6]

Hughes believes our identity as human beings 'depends on three things – a sense that one is unconditionally loved, a sense of one's own value, and a sense of meaning and purpose.'[7] Hughes goes on, 'This thirst in our souls, if not satisfied in God, lies behind most of the problems of the personality. Take almost any psychological problem and, when you cut your way through all the labels psychologists give to the various conditions, you come to a person who does not feel deeply loved, or who has little or no sense of worth, or feels there is no meaning or purpose to his or her life. Problems arise when we try to meet the deep needs of our souls outside of God.'[8]

Hughes believes that multitudes of Christians are in the position where they draw their life and strength not so much from God but from their dependency on a goal they believe they need to reach in order to make their lives work. 'People who continue to live this way, striving towards goals they erroneously believe will give them life and overcoming all the obstacles by sheer force of their own inner energy and strength, are extremely vulnerable to serious personal problems. One psychologist describes such people as preneurotic in the sense that, although they do not presently experience neurotic problems (excessive and debilitating emotions), they are candidates for such problems and can quickly tip over into neuroticism at any given moment.'[9]

Hundreds of thousands of Christians all over the world could be described as being in the preneurotic stage. Hughes appeals to Freud to explain his preneurotic theory. 'Freud was credited with the following statement (whether or not you agree with his psychology, his words make a lot of sense): "Neurosis is the exchange of one pain for another." Based on my own experience of dealing with people, I would add this: The pain of neurosis is a much easier pain to cope with and bear than the pain of feeling worthless, useless and purposeless ... The worst possible emotional feeling a person can experience is the feeling that one is unloved and has no point to being on the earth. That feeling is so devastating to the soul that it would tear it apart if there was not an unconscious mechanism designed to dampen those feelings and support the person through that trying period. Sometimes depression can be a defence against that devastation.'[10]

Freud's teaching on the unconscious is accepted by Hughes at face value. 'Much of our thinking takes place unconsciously. Mostly we are aware of what we are thinking, but our thinking goes on even when we are not aware of it ... Some believe we are influenced as much by our unconscious thoughts as those of which we are cognisant.'[11]

Hughes describes his psychological model like this. 'As long as a person reaches the goal he believes he needs to achieve security, signifi-cance and worth, he is unlikely to become a candidate for psychological problems. However, when he loses sight of that goal or gives up hope of reaching the goal, the unconscious can relieve the emotional pressure by depression. Many people never reach their desired goal. They never experience satisfaction ... Multitudes are living like this both inside and outside the church. But here's the danger. These people can easily become candidates for deeper emotional problems.'[12]

David Seamands

David Seamands is a big name in the Christian counselling move-ment. He was professor of Pastoral Ministries at the liberal Asbury Theological Seminary and pastor of the United Methodist Church. He was a pioneer in the field of Christian counselling and recognised as such at the 1992 Congress of Christian Counselling where, together with James Dobson, Larry Crabb and Gary Collins, he received the special 'Paraklesis' Award. He specialised in the type of counselling known as healing of the memories. His two books, *Healing for Damaged Emotions* (1981) and *Healing of Memories* (1985), are considered the 'inner-healer's bibles' by many in the Christian counselling movement.

Seamands believes that many sincere, Spirit-filled Christians have profound problems from which they need deliverance. In 1966, as a new pastor, he preached a sermon called 'The Holy Spirit and the Healing of Our Damaged Emotions'. After the service the former pastor, Dr Smith, confessed to Seamands, with tears in his eyes, that there was always a group of sincere people he could never help. 'I believe many of them were Spirit-filled Christians. But they had problems. They brought these things to me and I tried to help. But no amount of advice, no amount of Scripture or prayer on their part ever seemed to bring them lasting deliverance. I always felt guilty in my ministry, David. But I think you are onto something. Work on it, develop it. Please keep preaching it, for I believe what you have found is the answer.'[13]

Early in his pastoral experience Seamands discovered that the regular ministry of the church was not solving the problems of many people. 'Their problems were not being solved by the preaching of the Word, commitment to Christ, the filling of the Spirit, prayer, or the Sacraments.'[14] God showed him 'that ordinary ways of ministering would never help some problems'.[15] Seamands described these problems as 'damaged emotions' and 'unhealed memories' of past hurts. Even the new birth and being filled with the Spirit 'is not a shortcut to emotional health'.[16]

Seamands draws attention to the pressure of painful, repressed memories which produce psychological scars. 'Such scars have been buried in pain for so long that they are causing hurt and rage. And these scars are not touched by conversion and sanctifying grace, or by the ordinary benefits of prayer ... We preachers have often given people the mistaken idea that the new birth and being "filled with the Spirit" are going to automatically take care of these emotional hang-ups. But this isn't true. A great Crisis experience of Jesus Christ, as important and eternally valuable as this is, is not a shortcut to emotional health. It is not a quickie cure for personality problems ... There are people, like you and me, with hurts and scars and wrong programming that interfere with their present behaviour.'[17]

Seamands is very hard on Christians with what he calls a simplistic approach to those who have inner pain. The advice of these unsympathetic Christians is to read the Bible, to pray and to have more faith. 'However, people who say such things are being very cruel. They are only piling more weights on a person who is in pain and unsuccessfully struggling with an emotionally rooted problem. He already feels guilty about it; when people make him feel worse for even having the problem, they double the weight of his guilt and despair.'[18]

One of the most common damaged emotions is a deep sense of unworthiness, a continuous feeling of anxiety, inadequacy, and inferiority. 'What happens to this kind of person when he becomes a Christian?

Part of his mind believes in God's love, accepts God's forgiveness, and feels at peace for a while. Then all of a sudden everything within him rises up to cry out, "It's a lie! Don't believe it! Don't pray! There's no one up there to hear you. No one really cares. There's no one to relieve your anxiety. How could God possibly love you and forgive someone like you? You're too bad!" What has happened? The good news of the Gospel has not penetrated down into his damaged inner self, which also needs to be evangelised.'[19] Seamands appears to be saying that the new birth is not enough – a person also needs to have his damaged inner self evangelised through psychological counselling.

Low self-esteem, Seamands claims, is a weapon that Satan uses against Christians.[20] He argues that many of our deep emotional hurts are caused by our parents' poor behaviour. 'I am thinking of scores of young men and women who were fed a lot of false and harmful ideas by well-meaning but ignorant parents.'[21] By way of illustrating the way parents damage their children, Seamands relates the story of Shirley. Her father really did love her but repeatedly said to her, 'You know, you just can't make a peach out of a potato'. While her father thought he was helping her, he was really scarring and cutting at the very heart of her self-esteem. Seamands counselled Shirley and saw that the potato image had affected everything in her life, had made her as sensitive as an open wound. 'The hurts Shirley suffered were deep . . . I went out of my way to reprogramme her self-image . . . When she discovered she was a daughter of God, she let love and grace pour in and wash away all those potato feelings and potato images. It was one of the most remarkable changes I have ever seen.'[22]

According to Seamands, inner healing is necessary for Christians to feel God's grace. 'The realisation of grace cannot be maintained in some people without an inner healing of the past. God's care cannot be felt without a deep, inner healing of the past, God's care cannot be felt without a deep, inner reprogramming of all the bad conditioning that has been put into them by parents and family and teachers and preachers and the church.'[23] The idea that a Christian needs grace plus inner healing is contrary to Scripture. God promised Paul, 'My grace is sufficient for you, for My strength is made perfect in weakness' (2 Corinthians 12.9).

Here it is necessary to mention that David Seamands has admitted to having a long-term adulterous affair with a member of Wilmore United Methodist Church, where he had been pastor from 1962 to 1984. He apologised to his former church for what he termed 'a breach of trust and moral failure'.[24]

Larry Crabb

Larry Crabb is concerned about Christians who believe that 'sin has so blinded the hearts and minds of people that only truth from the Bible can bring the needed light. Study of God's Word therefore is a priority.'[25] These Christians rob the text of its relational and life-changing vitality. 'They would insist that proper exegesis of the Word never separates doctrine from practice, that the Word – understood, proclaimed, and obeyed – is itself sufficient to change lives.' But this approach, according to Crabb, is wishful thinking for it 'leaves large and significant areas of human experience untouched – and therefore unchanged'.[26]

Crabb is upset that many evangelical Christians do not accept Freud's teaching about the unconscious mind and therefore are unaware of the sin that lies below the waterline. The result is that 'while the church exhorts people to do what they consciously know to do, psychotherapists deal with the casualties of the church, people who sense that mysterious forces within are frustrating their efforts to obey.'[27] Evangelical Christians ignore the unconscious mind and minister only above the waterline by studying the Scriptures, proclaiming biblical truth, by teaching people the truths of the Christian faith and exhorting them to obey God's commandments, regardless of the emotions that they feel.[28] This approach leads to a shallow understanding of sin. If no work is done beneath the waterline, that is, in our unconscious mind, 'then work above the waterline results in a disastrous externalism in which visible conformity to local standards is all that matters. That community will be characterised by pressure, judgementalism, legalism and pride rather than by deep love for God and for others.'[29]

In *Inside Out* (1988) Crabb says that 'Christians are realising that their vision of church involvement, time in the Word, commitment to do right, claiming God's promises and surrendering to God's power is somehow not getting at the core of troubles of their hearts. We want more ... we know that our latest effort to follow Christ has left deep issues in our soul unaddressed. Is it possible to change at the core of our being?'[30] Crabb's plea is that we must have more. The Gospel is not enough; we need the Gospel plus an examination of our unconscious. Simply obeying God's Word does not deal with the issues below the waterline. Neither does the special work of the Holy Spirit. 'When blocks to growth are not overcome by more study or deeper yielding, some form of counselling sometimes seems appropriate.'[31] Crabb is sympathetic to the modern emphasis on counselling because most counsellors encourage an honest look below the waterline. He asserts that to live 'as God intends requires that we uncover the dirt and learn what we must do to participate in the cleaning process. We must take an inside look.'[32] Until Christians are willing and able to look at each other below the waterline, we need professional counsellors to promote deep change.[33] What Crabb is saying is that to deal with sin in the unconscious, Christians need psychotherapy.

Crabb teaches that all people, including Christians, have a deep thirst and inner pain that cannot be cured this side of Heaven. 'It is therefore not only okay to desire, *it is also okay to hurt*'[34] (his italics). Crabb explains that when we perceive that we are not respected, we hurt. Because we desperately desire what none of us has, 'there is an emptiness in the core of our being we simply do not want to face . . . We have all felt profoundly disappointed in every key relationship we've ever had. Therefore, we hurt.'[35] Crabb is highly irritated by some who teach that it is possible for Christians to experience a level of joy in Christ that swallows up all hurt.[36] Not so, Crabb asserts, all Christians have an incurable inner pain, and those who live as if they don't are simply in a state of denial, as Freud would say.

Gary Collins

Gary R. Collins is a prominent personality in the counselling movement. In 1991, he assumed responsibility for co-leading the fledgling American Association of Christian Counsellors (AACC). In the seven years that followed, he was AACC Executive Director and later President. Collins founded *Christian Counselling Today*, the official AACC magazine which he edited for several years. In 1998 he resigned from the AACC so that he could devote more time to developing Christian counselling and coaching worldwide. He is author of several books including *Christian Counselling: A Comprehensive Guide* (1988),

The Biblical Basis of Christian Counselling for People Helpers (1993) and *Christian Coaching: Helping Others Turn Potential into Reality* (2001).

Collins is a strong advocate for integrating Scripture and psychology. He says that the Bible never claims to be a textbook on counselling, for 'it was never meant to be God's sole revelation about helping people. In medicine, teaching and other "people-centred" helping fields, we have been permitted to learn much about God's creation through science and academic study. Why, then, should psychology be singled out as the one field that has nothing to contribute to the work of the counsellor?'[37]

Collins argues that God has permitted 'psychologists to develop careful research tools for studying human behaviour and professional journals for sharing these findings. As perhaps hundreds of thousands of people have come for help, professional counsellors have learned what makes people tick and how they can change.' Psychological research, according to Collins, has 'led to a vast reservoir of conclusions that are known to help counsellees and people who want to be effective people helpers.'

Collins says that he quotes research from social scientists 'on the assumption that all truth comes from God. He has revealed this truth through the Bible, God's written Word to human beings, but he has also permitted us to discover truth through experience and through the methods of scientific investigation . . . we limit our counselling effectiveness when we pretend that the discoveries of psychology have nothing to contribute to the understanding and solution of problems . . . let us accept the fact that psychology can be of great help to the Christian counsellor.'[38]

James Dobson of Focus on the Family

Dr James Dobson is the man more than any other who has brought the idea of self-esteem into the Christian church. He is the founder and president of Focus on the Family, and is heard on more than four thousand radio facilities around the world and publishes 11 magazines read by 3 million people each month. Dr Dobson has been a licensed psychologist and marriage, family, and child counsellor for around three decades.

Dobson propagated the importance of self-esteem in *Hide or Seek, How to Build Self-Esteem in Your Child* (1974). He wrote, 'The matter of personal worth is not only the concern of those who lack it. In a real sense, the health of an entire society depends on the ease with which its individual members can gain personal acceptance. Thus, whenever the keys to self-esteem are seemingly out of reach for a large percentage of the people, as in twentieth-century America, then widespread mental illness, neuroticism, hatred, alcoholism, drug abuse, violence, and social disorder will certainly occur. Personal worth is not something humans are free to take or leave. We must have it, and when it is unattainable, everybody suffers.'[39] Dobson makes the sweeping assertion that 'low self-esteem is a threat to the entire human family, affecting children, adolescents, the elderly, all socio-economic levels of society, and each race and ethnic culture.'[40] The secular and biblical views of self-esteem are dealt with in chapters 12, 13 and 14.

Conclusion

The Christian counselling movement is highly irritated by those who believe in the sufficiency of Christ to live a life worthy of the Gospel, who believe that there is no condemnation to those who are in Christ, who believe that Christians are more than conquerors through Christ who loved us *(Romans 8)*. Not so, say the counsellors, for their under-lying presupposition is that Christians need more than the Gospel to overcome life's problems. Major problems that require counselling are the sins that lie buried in the recesses of our unconscious mind, the problem of inner pain and the problem of low self-esteem which leads to depression. Because Christians cannot overcome these problems simply by obeying God, reading the Bible and praying, we need the interventions offered by counselling.

4
Integrating Psychological and Biblical Truth

A KEY POINT to emerge from the first three chapters is that mainstream Christian counselling is based on an integration model that attempts to incorporate the best of secular psychology with biblical teaching. The idea of integrating psychology and biblical wisdom was first proposed by Clyde Narramore in the early 1960s, as we saw in chapter 1. He claimed that pulpit preaching was not enough to deal with the serious emotional problems that are common in church congregations. He believed that counselling based on psychological principles helped Christians to deal with the problems of everyday living.

Two decades later John Carter and Bruce Narramore, in *The Integration of Psychology and Theology* (1979), asserted that 'both psychology and theology offer a great deal toward an understanding of the human race'.[1] Their support for integration is based on the belief that all truth is God's truth, wherever it is found.[2] 'Given this unity of truth, it is possible to integrate truth arrived at from different sources and with different methodologies.'[3] Reason, revelation, and the scientific method all are seen as playing a valid role in the search for truth.[4] A funda-mental assumption that underpins the integrationist position is that the facts of psychology are based on true scientific investigation. A survey among psychologists teaching at Christian colleges and universities found *The Integration of Psychology and Theology* to be an extremely influential book (Staff, 1987).

Fuller Theological Seminary promotes integration

Fuller Theological Seminary has played a pivotal role in the ongoing process of integrating psychology and the Christian faith. The main purpose of Fuller's School of Psychology, established in 1965, is to encourage the discovery of new connections between the Christian faith and the disciplines of psychology. By placing the cross of Jesus Christ at the heart of psychological education, Fuller 'continues to prepare a distinctive kind of clinical psychologist: women and men whose under-standings and actions are deeply informed by both psychology and the Christian faith'. Fuller's integrative approach is built on the conviction that Christians with clinical and evaluation skills will help people on their journeys toward wholeness. The clinical psychology course at Fuller aims to meld psychology and theology in clinical practice.[5]

Fuller explains that the integration of psychology and theology is an attempt to bring the Christian faith to bear on the practice of psychology. 'What does theology have to say to psychology? What difference does belief in God make in the way a psychotherapist assists a troubled indi-vidual or family? In what way is Christ the answer to human need? How can the life of the church be a context for healing? What is the role of the Holy Spirit in the healing process?'

According to Fuller, 'psychologists have reflected carefully on the nature of human experience, the nature of family conflict, the effects of violence, depression, anger, severe mental illness, burnout and a range of other issues. One aspect of integration is an attempt to respond to these questions. Throughout the history of the church, there are individuals and communities that have wrestled with the Christian's relationship to the larger culture. Our efforts at integration would do well to be sensi-tive to how others before us have done so.'

Fuller's approach is to help students to reflect upon the ways in which information from both disciplines can be fused. Students are encouraged to develop their own synergy of psychology and theology in clinical practice. Fuller's Integration Library, which houses its special collection of books and research papers, is an indication of its commitment to fostering the relationship between psychology and theology.

Integrating psychological excellence and biblical truth

The American Association of Christian Counsellors (AACC) has always been deeply committed to the integration of biblical and psychological truth. In 1993 Gary Collins, who was the head of the Association at the time, ran an advertisement in *Christianity Today* (the 17/5/93 issue) which emphasised its support for integration: 'The AACC is made up of nearly 5,000 professional, pastoral, and lay counsellors who are equally committed to psychological excellence and biblical truth. Members of the AACC seek to encourage the integration of counselling principles with biblical theology.'

We have already seen that the counselling scene in the UK is strongly integrationist. Both CWR and the London School of Theology (LST) follow an integration model. Selwyn Hughes demonstrates a clear commitment to combining biblical truth with the principles of secular psychology. The London School looks beyond the Bible to understand human beings. 'Just as Christian doctors need more than the Bible to understand physical function and dysfunction, so Christian counsellors need all the insights that can be gained from secular study of the psyche. We seek to "integrate" such insights into a Christian understanding of people, and so our model is an "Integrative Christian Therapy".'[6] Most Christian counsellors in the UK offer a wide range of psychological approaches. The Watford Christian Counselling Service, which is operated by LST, explains that it uses an integrative model that incorporates aspects of psychodynamic therapy (based on Freudian concepts), narrative therapy (based on Michael White's belief that there are no absolute truths but only socially sanctioned points of view), and Rational Emotive Behaviour Therapy (based on the psychological theories of Albert Ellis).[7]

In his book *Effective Biblical Counselling* Larry Crabb described his method of integration as 'Spoiling the Egyptians'.[8] In Crabb's metaphor the 'Egyptians' represent secular psychological theories – his spoiling technique aims to take the best from secular psychological theories and combine them with biblical wisdom. Crabb argues that if a counsellor will 'carefully screen' concepts from psychology he will be able to determine their 'compatibility with Christian presuppositions'. He claims that his method enables the church to glean 'useful insights' from psychology without compromising its commitment to Scripture.

To illustrate how secularists might have something to offer Christianity, Crabb writes: 'Man is responsible (Glasser) to believe truth which will result in responsible behaviour (Ellis) that will provide him with meaning, hope (Frankl), and love (Fromm) and will serve as a guide (Adler) to effective living with others as a self- and other-accepting person (Harris), who understands himself (Freud), who appropriately expresses himself (Perls), and who knows how to control himself (Skinner).'[9] Crabb is particularly impressed with Carl Rogers' contribution to relationship counselling[10] and writes, 'Christians would do well to read Carl Rogers on the need for profoundly accepting the client as a worthwhile human being.'[11] Amazing really, that in Crabb's eyes Albert Ellis is the model for responsible behaviour; that a Christian needs to read Carl Rogers to learn how to treat people; that Erich Fromm's humanistic philosophy can teach a Christian about the meaning of love.

Mainstream Christian counselling seeks to integrate the best parts of Sigmund Freud's psychotherapy, Alfred Adler's goal-orientated counselling, Carl Rogers' client-centred counselling, Albert Ellis' Rational Emotive Behavioural Therapy and Abraham Maslow's needs-related psychology, into its armoury. For example, the Meier Clinics, who claim to be one of the most trusted names in Christian counselling, 'integrate biblically-based, Christian beliefs with psychological principles to treat the whole person – mental, emotional, physical and spiritual. Our total commitment to Christian counselling as well as sound clinical training distinguishes our approach.'[12]

Psychological truth and God's truth

Crucial to the integration model is the assumption that biblical truth and psychological 'truth' can be combined to produce 'all truth'. We are asked to accept that the psychological theories of men have acquired a standard of truth that allows them to stand alongside God's revealed, eternal Word. Based upon this presupposition, the Christian counselling movement has integrated psychological theory and biblical revelation to form a unified view of human nature and how to solve human problems. Yet psychological 'truths' are continually changing, whereas biblical truth never changes. The integrationists are on dangerous ground when they seek to integrate God's truth, as revealed in Scripture, with 'man's truth', as currently understood and taught from outside the Scriptures. The statement – 'All truth is God's truth' – has a dangerous tendency, for it tends to put all 'truth' on the same level. It claims that what is currently believed to be 'true' through science or psychology is just as surely true as biblical truth.

It is sad that some Christians are reinterpreting the Scriptures because modern psychological theory has apparently unearthed some new 'truth'. Some Christians search the Scriptures to seek support for their favourite psychological theory. As we shall see in chapter 11, Larry Crabb uses verses from *Romans 8* to support Freud's theory of an unconscious mind. The Bible is no longer the primary source of truth, but a secondary source, and is used to support the secular psychologists' version of 'truth'.

Scripture teaches that God's words are truth itself – they are the final standard and definition of truth. So Jesus can say to the Father, 'Your word is truth' *(John 17.17)*. God's words are not only true but *the* truth. This means that God's word is the final standard by which truth is to be judged. God's truth is revealed in Jesus Christ (I am the truth) and the written Word of God (God's word is truth). Christ said that everyone who is of the truth hears his voice *(John 18.37)*. The church of the living God is the custodian of God's truth on earth *(1 Timothy 3.15)*. God's absolute and unchangeable truth deals with that which is spiritual, moral and eternal. God's Word teaches us everything that we need to know about the spiritual and moral condition of man.

God's common grace

Another argument used to integrate secular psychological techniques into the church is that of common grace. The talking therapies are part of God's common grace that bring blessing to all mankind, according to an article in *Evangelicals Now* (October 2008). Dr Mike Davies and Charles H. Whitworth write: 'The talking therapies such as Cognitive

Behaviour Therapy (CBT) should not be dismissed because the models used are secular and not specifically Christian. A biblical understanding of common grace means that insights into human behaviour and health are often granted to non-Christians. In our experience as a GP practice, rightly used, the techniques derived from CBT can be very helpful in moderating the symptoms of what are often very debilitating conditions.'[13] Dr Davies asserts that cognitive therapy is part of God's common grace on the basis of his experience in general practice. Apparently his experience has given special insight that enables him to identify those therapies which are part of God's common grace, and therefore good for all mankind.

On the basis of the common grace argument we are asked to believe that the talking therapies that have been developed by Albert Ellis and Aaron Beck (cognitive therapy) are part of God's blessing to all mankind.

To test the validity of the integrationist approach we must examine the psychological theories that the Christian counselling movement accept as 'truth' and part of God's common grace in the light of Scripture. We need to dig deeper so that we understand what is being propagated as psychological truth by the integrationists. We must now turn to the giants of psychology – Sigmund Freud, Alfred Adler, Abraham Maslow, Carl Rogers and Albert Ellis. The question in mind, as we examine their theories, is this: Do the theories of these men, which have been integrated into Christian counselling, constitute truth? We need also to be open to the alternative explanation that the integration of Scripture and psychological 'truth' is introducing dangerous false teaching into the church.

5
Sigmund Freud – the Founding Father of Psychotherapy

THE IDEA that we need psychotherapy to overcome our problems of daily living really started with Sigmund Freud. His influence on Western thought in general, and psychological theory in particular, has been so great that it is impossible to understand the Christian counselling movement without first understanding the Freudian approach to psychotherapy. Freud's concept of the unconscious is woven into the very fabric of Christian counselling. We have already seen that Larry Crabb accepts at face value Freud's teaching on the unconscious. Crabb freely acknowledges that Freud introduced the idea of psychodynamics to the modern mind. He writes, 'I believe that [Freud's] psychodynamic theory is both provocative and valuable in recognising elements in the human personality that many theologians have failed to see.'[1] As we shall see in chapter 11, Crabb has a deep commitment to Freudian psychology.

Selwyn Hughes, doyen of the British Christian counselling movement, has found Freud's theory of the unconscious very helpful in his counselling ministry. He speaks of 'an unconscious mechanism designed to dampen' devastating feelings of the soul that would tear us apart,[2] and explains that for years he has 'spent a lot of time digging into people's pasts in order to find an explanation for their behaviour'.[3] In the previous chapter we saw that the Watford Christian Counselling Service, which has a close association with the London School of Theology, uses an integrative model of counselling that incorporates aspects of Freud's psychodynamic therapy.

In *Happiness is a Choice* (1994), Christian psychiatrists Minirth and Meier explain that in their practice they see humans who are 'dominated by their own unconscious drives, conflicts, motives . . . But a wise counsellor will try to look into the individual's heart – his unconscious thoughts and emotions – to see what that individual can do to quit bringing on his own precipitating stresses.'[4] They believe that *Jeremiah 17.9* is the key to Christian psychiatry: 'The heart is deceitful above all things, and desperately wicked; who can know it?' They claim that 'the prophet Jeremiah is saying that we humans cannot fathom or comprehend how desperately sinful and deceitful our hearts are – our unconscious motives, conflicts, drives, emotions and thoughts.'[5] The therapeutic approach of Minirth and Meier is based on Freud's theory of the unconscious.

The philosophy of Sigmund Freud (1856-1939)

Freud was the man with a clear agenda who founded the worldwide movement for psychotherapy. The essential idea behind Freudian psychology is that, to a large degree, human behaviour is controlled by our unconscious mind. The aim of psychotherapy is to delve into the unconscious in order to offer a way of escape from the murky waters that lie deeply hidden.

Freud's voluminous writings have had a massive influence on Western thought. He took up the baton of promoting an amoral worldview from Nietzsche, the philosopher who pronounced the death of God. He wrote that Nietzsche was a 'philosopher whose guesses and intuitions often agree in the most astonishing way with the laborious findings of psychoanalysis'.[6] Freud was also attracted to Darwin's theories of evolution 'for they held out hopes of an extraordinary advance in our understanding of the world'.[7] Evolutionary doctrine profoundly altered the prevailing conception of man. The scriptural view of man, created in the image of God and possessing an immortal soul, was under challenge. Man was now seen as being part of the animal world, differing from other non-human animals only in degree of structural complexity. This made it possible, for the first time, to treat man as an object of scientific investigation. The pseudoscience of psychology could now explain the human condition and psychotherapy was seen as a useful technique for improving behaviour.

Freud claimed the ability to delve into the hidden depths of the unconscious mind. He also claimed to have uncovered the secrets of human sexual behaviour that had eluded mankind for thousands of years. He described an Oedipus complex which saw children as sexual beings. According to Freud, boys concentrate their sexual wishes upon their mother and develop hostile impulses against their father as a rival, while girls adopt an analogous attitude. At the centre of Freud's thinking was his hostility to the Christian faith, and his motivation was to provide an interpretation of human sexuality that disregarded biblical morality. Freud gathered around him a set of disciples who were committed to his radical ideas and determined to spread the Freudian worldview through the techniques of psychoanalysis. The influence of Freud has been pervasive and far-reaching. His psychoanalytic movement has spread Freudian philosophy across the Western world,[8] and through the ministry of the Christian counselling movement, into the Christian church.

Freud, cocaine and the devil

The popular view is that Freud adopted a scientific approach to the investigation of human behaviour. What is not widely known is that Freud used cocaine and had a deep interest in the occult. In his book *Sigmund Freud's Christian Unconscious* Paul Vitz deals with Freud's cocaine habit. 'Freud began experimenting with the drug in 1884, when he was 28, at a time when cocaine was almost unknown in scientific circles. During the period 1884-1887, Freud took cocaine frequently, sometimes in heavy doses. After taking the drug himself and getting some preliminary reports from others, Freud published glowing descriptions of cocaine.'[9]

Freud had a deep interest in matters related to the devil. In *Sigmund Freud and the Jewish Mystical Tradition*, David Bakan describes how

Freud surrounded himself with every heathen god he could find. He had the habit of taking one or other piece from his collection and examining it by sight and touch while he was talking to his colleagues. 'As if in sheer spite he pursued "idols" and their associated trappings with a deep fascination. His study and consulting room bulged with them. Sachs tells of the early meetings at Freud's quarters, how "under the silent stare of idols and animal-shaped gods, we listened to some new article by Freud or read and discussed our own products or just talked about things that interested us".'[10] Bakan argues that the devil had his role to play in Freud's development. 'The devil stands opposed to the Mosaic features incorporated in Christianity. Freud once remarked to his associates, "Do you know that I am the devil? All my life I have had to play the devil, in order that others would be able to build the most beautiful cathedral with the materials that I produced."'[11]

The research of Peter Swales suggests that Freud made a pact with the devil. According to Vitz, 'Now the devil comes into all this through two facts, whose importance Peter Swales has recognised and which he brought to my attention. The Swalesian theory is thus the third published interpretation of a Freudian pact with the devil.'[12] Vitz concludes 'that cocaine for Freud was thoroughly linked to the devil, and, indeed, was connected from the beginning to some kind of pact. Thus, while Freud was still a young physician – years before the beginning of psychoanalysis, and some 10-12 years before the psychological "pact" that Bakan proposes – he was already very strongly involved with the devil. The exact nature of the pact is still not clear, but it appears to have been modelled on Faust's pact . . . '[13, 14]

Vitz argues that if we look back on Freud's life it is apparent that the issues of Heaven and (especially) Hell, of the devil and damnation, were deeply connected to his personal motivation. 'The evidence cited here makes a strong case that a very important part of Freud sided with Satan against God and Heaven and Christ, and sided with the enemies of the church.'[15] After explaining the significance of the Anti-Christ, Vitz claims, 'the possibility that Freud saw himself, at least in certain aspects, as the Anti-Christ must be taken seriously'.[16] A proper evaluation of Freud's theories must take account of his involvement with the occult, for it undoubtedly influenced his view of the human condition.

Freud's unconscious

The concept of the unconscious is Freud's great contribution to psychological theory. He claimed that humans suppress unwanted and painful memories in their unconscious mind. The uncovering and exposure of the mysterious contents of the unconscious became the foundation of psychoanalysis. The concept of the unconscious continues largely unchallenged to this day and is the bedrock of most forms of psychotherapeutic counselling, and as we shall see, is an essential component of the Christian counselling movement in the UK and the USA and elsewhere.

Freud developed the theory that human unconsciousness is a powerful determinant of our thinking, feelings and behaviour. He saw the unconscious as a permanent repository of all our perceptions, experiences, emotions and repressed stages of development. It is a submerged iceberg of hidden urges, feelings, passions and ideas that are tied to anxiety, conflict and pain. So the majority of what we experience in our lives – the underlying emotions, beliefs, feelings, and impulses – are not available to us at a conscious level, for most of what drives human behaviour lies concealed in our unconscious. These feelings and thoughts influence our actions and our conscious awareness.

The contents of the unconscious cannot be made available voluntarily, according to Freud. We need a psychoanalyst to do this! Freud claimed that by the use of certain counselling techniques, such as free association, hypnosis, the interpretation of dreams, and recollection of memories, a psychotherapist could uncover and analyse the unconscious. The therapist could then explain the reasons for neurotic behaviour and free the patient from the tyrannical control of their unconscious mind. It follows that the only real cure for human problems is a deep analysis of the unconscious by a psychotherapist.

Freud's theory of the unconscious is extremely subtle, for it places enormous power in the hands of the therapist, for only he has the esoteric knowledge needed to delve into the deepest recesses of our unconscious mind and interpret its motivations. And, of course, it is impossible to prove that the unconscious does not exist, for how does one prove a negative? The implication of Freud's theory is that unhappy, miserable people are now at the mercy of the psychotherapist. In 1913

Otto Gross, Austrian psychoanalyst and early disciple of Freud who later became an anarchist, wrote, 'The psychology of the unconscious is the philosophy of the revolution . . . It is called upon to enable an inner freedom, called upon as preparation for the revolution.'[17]

The *Internet Encyclopedia of Philosophy* interprets Freud's theory of the unconscious as highly deterministic. He was 'arguably the first thinker to apply deterministic principles systematically to the sphere of the mental, and to hold that the broad spectrum of human behaviour is explicable only in terms of the (usually hidden) mental processes or states which determine it.' Freud attributed significance to slips of the tongue or pen, obsessive behaviour, and dreams for they reveal in covert form what would otherwise not be known. He suggested that freedom of the will is tightly circumscribed, for the choices we make are governed by hidden mental processes of which we are unaware and over which we have no control.[18]

We must understand that the unconscious mind is a construct developed by Freud's unregenerate, darkened imagination. Psychoanalysis depends on the postulate of an unconscious, and without it, the whole edifice collapses. Yet it can never be proved or disproved, and does not even qualify as a scientific hypothesis. Its contribution to the understanding of the human condition is of no real worth.

In *The Memory Wars* (1995) Professor Frederick Crews convincingly dismantles the entire Freudian enterprise, from beginning to end. As a one time supporter of Freud, he describes his pathway to enlightenment. 'Only much later did it dawn on me that psychoanalysis is the paradigmatic pseudoscience of our epoch – one that deserves to be addressed not in the thrifty spirit of "What can we salvage from Freud?" but rather with principled attention to its faulty logic, its manufacturing of its own evidence, and its facile explanation of adult behaviour by reference to unobservable and arbitrarily posited childhood fantasy.'[19] Crews claims that Freud's therapeutic successes appear to be nonexistent, and that he lied about them. Freud's psychotherapeutic movement conducted itself less like a scientific-medical enterprise than like a politburo, bent on snuffing out any criticism. The 'science' that Freud invented 'was, and remains, a pseudoscience, in that it relies on unexamined dogma, lacks any safeguards against the drawing of arbitrary inferences, and insulates itself in several ways from the normal give-and-take of scientific debate'.[20] Freud's dynamic unconscious turns out to be 'a morass of contradictions'.[21] Crews concludes that Freud 'has been the most overrated figure in the entire history of science and medicine – one who wrought immense harm through the propagation of false aetiologies, mistaken diagnoses, and fruitless lines of inquiry'.[22]

Freud and Christianity

Underlying all Freud's thinking was a deep hostility to the Christian faith. In a letter to his colleague Wilhelm Fliess, Freud describes how deeply upset he was by the Christian influence he perceived during a visit to Rome. Freud was disturbed by its meaning and incapable of putting out of his mind his own misery and all the other misery which he knew to exist. 'I found almost intolerable the lie of the salvation of mankind which rears its head so proudly to heaven.'[23] This intense dislike of Christianity produced in Freud an inner conviction, 'the pursuit of which became the dominant, but covert, aim of his life – to expose the "lie of salvation" and show it to be just that, a lie'.[24]

In his book, *Freud – An introduction to his life and work*, Isbister concludes that Freud hated Christianity and 'all that it stood for – anti-Semitism; the hypocrisy of "Christian" civilisation; the stern demands of its morality; and the suggestion that man's destiny was ultimately linked with an eternal purpose. From 1900, his opposition to Christianity, hitherto mostly expressed as caustic comments in his letters, found an increasing outlet in his theories and in the movement they spawned . . . Freud's overt aims may well have been scientific – furthering the new science of depth psychology – but his covert aims were far more subtle and complex – to conquer the source (as he saw it) of Christianity, Rome, to accomplish that which Hannibal failed to . . . the covert aspects of his mission become clearer as the history of the psychoanalytic movement unfolds.'[25]

Conclusion

Freud was no friend of the Christian faith. Indeed, the unspoken motivation behind much of his work was a passion to subvert the Christian Gospel. There is no doubt that his fascination with the occult influenced the development of his model of psychotherapy. His theory of the unconscious is in direct conflict with the biblical view of man as created in the image of God and responsible for his thoughts, words and actions. Freud's theory made the unconscious mind the driving force behind human behaviour, thereby creating a victim mentality, for we all are victims of the unconscious.

Freud's theory of the unconscious places humans into tyrannical bondage, for we are controlled by an inner force of which we are unaware, over which we have no control and which we cannot even begin to understand. Our bad behaviour and neurotic actions are controlled by unconscious forces and all that we can do is place our faith in Freud and his disciples. The psychoanalyst has great power for he alone has the esoteric knowledge and skill to uncover and interpret our unconscious motivations, he alone can interpret human behaviour, and he alone can open the door to salvation from the deep inner pain that resides in our unconscious mind. And who can question the counsel of the psychotherapist?

The claim that the psychotherapist can delve into our unconscious mind is contrary to the teachings of Scripture, which teaches that God alone knows the mind of man. 'For what man knows the things of a man except the spirit of the man which is in him?' *(1 Corinthians 2.11.)* King Solomon prayed, 'You alone know the hearts of the sons of men' *(2 Chronicles 6.30)*. Jesus knew the thoughts of the Pharisees *(Matthew 9.4)*. It is God who tests the mind, who gives to each person according to his ways *(Jeremiah 17.9-10)*. The word of God is a 'discerner of the thoughts and intents of the heart' *(Hebrews 4.12)*. The plain message of the Bible is that it is not possible for a human being to know what is in the mind of another person.

This is why psychotherapy is such a fraud, for it can never uncover the real thoughts of a man. 'But the natural man [that is the therapist] does not receive the things of the Spirit of God, for they are foolishness to him; nor can he know them, because they are spiritually discerned' *(1 Corinthians 2.14)*. The therapist only knows what the client chooses to tell him, and he has no way of knowing if the client is telling the truth, or saying things that he wants the therapist to hear. Only God knows the thoughts of a man.

A fundamental error of the Freudian theory of human behaviour is that it does not recognise the true nature of fallen man. Rather, it helps a man to avoid the consequences of his sin, and by labelling him as a victim to mental illness, it fixes him in his sin. Instead of repentance and righteous living, Freud's psychoanalysis delves into our past and shifts the blame for our sinful behaviour on to someone else, usually our parents. It is not difficult to see that Freud's system of psychotherapy is in direct conflict with biblical truth. The Bible teaches that all humans are in bondage to sin – not to their unconscious. Sin, and all manner of evil, comes from the heart of man, not from our unconscious. We choose sin when we are drawn away by our own desires and lusts. The remedy is the Cross of Christ, not psychotherapy. The Christian is united with Christ in his death, 'that the body of sin might be done away with, that we should no longer be slaves of sin' *(Romans 6.6)*. The Christian is 'dead indeed to sin, but alive to God in Christ Jesus our Lord' *(Romans 6.11)*.

The Christian counselling movement, that freely uses the technique of psychoanalysis, is asking us to accept that Freud's theory of the unconscious is founded on psychological truth. The church is being persuaded to believe that Christians benefit from the integration of Freud's teaching with Scripture.

6
The Individual Psychology of Alfred Adler

ALFRED ADLER (1870-1937) is recognised as the grandfather of humanistic psychology. He was a member of Freud's Vienna Circle until he left because of irreconcilable differences. After Adler broke from the group he developed a holistic approach to psychotherapy, which aims to treat the individual within the context of his environment and which focuses on the goals and purposes of human behaviour. He was an existentialist in the vein of Nietzsche and Camus, believing that life was inherently purposeless. Nevertheless a purposeless life could still have meaning, so long as it was self-chosen by the individual. He believed that the most basic human drive is the desire to overcome an initial state of inadequacy and move to a position of power. He called his system of psychotherapy Individual Psychology.

At the heart of Adlerian psychology is the idea that all people are always striving toward a goal of significance. As we have seen, Selwyn Hughes acknowledges the influence of Adler in his counselling ministry.[1] Hughes writes, 'The psychologist, Adler, made the point that the best way to understand any unit of behaviour is to ask yourself:

What is the goal to which the behaviour is directed?' He acknowledges that 'one of the most helpful insights I have ever discovered in my counselling ministry is that all behaviour moves towards a goal ... Behind most problems is an unrecognised wrong goal. And most of the work in counselling is helping a person discover that goal.'[2]

Here Hughes was referring to Alfred Adler's dominant idea that human behaviour is driven by a final 'fictional' goal that resides in the unconscious. This goal develops in early childhood and although we are sometimes unaware of our 'fictional' goal it nevertheless has a profound effect on our future behaviour. The aim of Adler's psychotherapy is to uncover the 'fictional' goal and move it in a more realistic direction.

Childhood memories

Adler believed that dysfunction in childhood must be addressed to alleviate individual suffering. He claimed that factors such as pampering and neglect, as well as birth order had an impact on personality problems. These factors shape how children perceive themselves, or shape the story they tell themselves about themselves. By age five this story, or 'fiction', has become fixed in their minds, and will henceforth be the framework through which the child interprets and responds to future events. Adler called the story that we tell ourselves (much of it unconscious) a 'fiction', to distinguish it from the reality of a person's life.

These childhood fictions govern the way we see the world, ourselves and the very choices we make. Adler felt that if the individual could be helped to identify the fictions that were causing problems, and helped to develop a self-image and goal, he would have a happier, more productive life. The role of the analyst is to gather information on a patient's dreams, statements about relationships and childhood traumas. Over time the analyst is able to understand the original 'fiction' that is causing problems and devise a plan for getting the patient back on track.

Inferiority complex

It is from Adler that we get the term 'inferiority complex'. This arose out of his view that as babies and young children, much of our emotional life is a compensation for a sense of inferiority. Adler believed that humans are motivated primarily by their overwhelming desire to overcome a feeling of inferiority, developed during childhood, and to gain power. He argued that each individual strives for what he called 'superiority'. In this he was profoundly influenced by Nietzsche's notions of striving and self-creation. Adler's striving for superiority was a forerunner for what later became known as 'self-realisation' or 'self-actualisation'. The human potential movement and humanistic psychology (Abraham Maslow, Carl Rogers, Rollo May, etc) owe a great debt to Adler for developing this line of thought.[3]

Goal orientated

Alfred Adler wrote that every psychological activity shows that its direction is governed by a predetermined goal. 'However, soon after a child's psychological development starts, all these tentative, individually recognisable goals, come under the dominance of the fictitious goal, a finale that is regarded as firmly established . . . This insight into any personality that can be derived from Individual Psychology leads us to an important concept: If we are to understand the nature of an individual, then every psychological manifestation should be perceived and understood as only preparatory for a particular goal. Everyone develops a final goal, either consciously or unconsciously, but ignorant of its meaning.'[4]

Although the final goal represents a subjective, fictional view of the future, it is what guides the person in the present.[5] Dr Henry Stein, Director of the Alfred Adler Institute, explains, 'Depending on the individual's unconscious, fictional final goal, and feeling of inferiority, one need would be pursued "as if" it were primary. An exaggerated goal of personal superiority, security and significance (originally adopted in childhood) could intoxicate an individual with the illusion of an intensified "need" that they believe could only be satisfied in a specific, concrete form. Classical Adlerian psychotherapy attempts to trace these mistaken ideas about security and significance, back to childhood, and then correct them. In psychotherapy, it is fascinating to see how clients' "felt needs" change after they recognise and give up a dysfunctional goal.'[6]

The problem with Adler

Although Adler eventually broke away from Freud, there is no doubt that he was strongly influenced by the Freudian view of man. While he did not give the unconscious the same emphasis as Freud, he nevertheless believed that many of our actions and behaviour are influenced by unconscious forces. The idea that factors in childhood lead us to adopt a 'fictional' life goal of which we are unaware, but that has an enormous influence on our behaviour, is highly deterministic. According to Adler, we are victims of our childhood, and therefore not accountable for our actions. And, like Freud, it is only the analyst that can uncover our 'fictional' goal, and then point us in the right direction. But why should we place our faith in the analyst who probably has a 'fictional' goal of his own?

Scripture teaches that the Word of God is a two-edged sword that pierces the human heart and spirit, discerning the thoughts and intents of the heart *(Hebrews 4.12)*. It sheds light on human motives and desires, and reveals sin. The unregenerate human heart is a slave to sin, not to a 'fictional' final goal. The idea that a Christian, regenerated by the Holy Spirit, has a 'fictional' final goal of which he is unaware is itself pure fiction. We know whom we have believed and are committed to doing his will, and witnessing to the truth of his Gospel. It seems strange that an experienced Christian man like Selwyn Hughes should adopt the philosophy of Alfred Adler to counsel brothers and sisters in Christ. Why does he not rely on God's Word?

7

Abraham Maslow – the Man with New Age Tendencies

A BRAHAM MASLOW (1908-1970) was one of the founders of humanistic psychology. As a young man he studied psychology at the University of Wisconsin where he found a mentor in Alfred Adler. He continued his studies at Brooklyn College in New York, and in 1951 was appointed professor of psychology at Brandeis University. He became recognised as the leader of the humanistic school of psychology that emerged in the 1950s and 1960s, which he referred to as the 'third force' – a force beyond Freudian psychotherapy and Skinner's behaviourism. While Maslow coined the term 'the third force' for humanistic psychology, he saw something on the horizon which he called the 'fourth force', which has become known as transpersonal psychology with a strong New Age element. His influence continues to be felt in the fields of health, education, and the burgeoning counselling industry. He died of a heart attack in 1970.

Maslow introduced a new way of thinking to psychology, for he wanted to know what constituted positive mental health, rather than continuing to focus on mental illness. Humanistic psychology was based on the idea that people possess the inner resources for growth and healing and that the aim of therapy is to help remove obstacles to achieving this.

Maslow's interest in spiritual matters

Maslow was openly hostile to traditional biblical Christianity. In his book *Religions, Values, and Peak-Experience* (1964) he claims that the truly religious are those who have mystical peak-experiences. However, those who live by sound doctrine and try to obey God's moral law are the enemy of true religion. 'The mystic experience, the illumination, the great awakening, along with the charismatic seer who started the whole thing, are forgotten, lost, or transformed into their opposites.'[1] Maslow argues that organised religion and the churches are the major enemies of the true religious experience.

Larry Crabb, in his book *Effective Biblical Counselling*, explains why he bases his theory of sanctification on the psychological model of Abraham Maslow. He writes, 'Abraham Maslow's classical need hierarchy suggests that human beings have five basic needs. The lowest one in the hierarchy must be met before the person is motivated to meet the second need and so on up the hierarchy . . . Maslow's listing also suggests (and I tend to agree) that security or love is a more basic need than purpose or significance. However, both are required before I will be motivated to truly express who I am, simply because until I enjoy security and significance, I do not believe I really am anyone.'[2] Crabb claims that 'self-actualisation, the ultimate and highest need in Maslow's system, comes close to the biblical concept of becoming mature in Christ.'[3]

Maslow, like Crabb, has a deep interest in spiritual matters. He sees a spiritual road which can be travelled together by all who are not afraid of truth, by theists and non-theists alike. He believes that everything that defines the characteristic of the religious experience can be accepted as real by clergymen and atheists. 'What remains of disagreement? Only, it seems, the concept of supernatural beings or of supernatural laws or forces; and I must confess my feeling that . . . this difference doesn't seem to be of any great consequence except for the comfort of the individual himself . . . ' Maslow asserts that 'increasingly, leading theologians, and sophisticated people in general, define their god, not as a person, but as a force, a principle, a gestalt-quality of the whole of Being, an integrating power that expresses the unity and therefore the meaningfulness of the cosmos.'[4] Clearly, the God of the Bible has no place in Maslow's religious experience.

His theories of human nature have had an enormous impact on how both secular society and the Christian counselling movement view human problems and needs. In his paper on a theory of human motivation Maslow describes a human being as a wanting (thirsty) animal that desires to be satisfied. Deeply opposed to the biblical view of man created in the image of God, Maslow developed the image of a wanting, thirsty man whose chief purpose in life is to satisfy his needs.

Maslow's worldview

Maslow was well aware that his motivational model of human behaviour was part of a larger worldview. In the preface to the second edition of *Toward a Psychology of Being* (1968) he described humanist psychology as 'one facet of a general Weltanschauung, a new philosophy of life, a new conception of man'. Based on his observations of human nature, he makes the arrogant claim that his psychology, not Scripture, can produce a system of moral absolutes. He believed that if his assumptions about human nature are proven true, 'they promise a scientific ethic, a natural value system, a court of ultimate appeal for the determination of good and bad, of right and wrong. The more we learn about man's natural tendencies, the easier it will be to tell him how to be good, how to be happy, how to be fruitful, how to respect himself, how to love, how to fulfil his highest potentialities.'[5]

Maslow's worldview depends on the central idea that the highest values reside within the human heart. This he acknowledges 'is in sharp contradiction to the older and more customary beliefs that the highest values can come only from a supernatural God, or from other sources outside human nature itself'.[6] Again, Maslow makes it clear that there is no place for the God of the Bible in his thinking. Here we are dealing with a man who sees himself as a secular prophet who will deliver modern man from the tyranny of traditional religion and lead us to the promised land of human self-actualisation. He wants us to believe that his so-called 'scientific' psychological observations will evolve into a new value system that teaches mankind how to be good and happy.

An optimistic view of human nature

Maslow was optimistic about human nature. 'This inner nature, as much as we know of it so far, seems not to be intrinsically or primarily evil ... Human nature is not nearly as bad as it has been thought to be. In fact it can be said that the possibilities of human nature have customarily been sold short. Since this inner nature is good or neutral rather than bad, it is best to bring it out and to encourage it rather than to suppress it. If it is permitted to guide our life, we grow healthy, fruitful, and happy.'[7] Here Maslow is directly contradicting the teaching of Scripture – that the heart of man is desperately sinful.

Maslow believes that evil is reactive, a response to bad treatment by others. He claims that psychotherapy reduces evil and 'changes its quality into "healthy" self-affirmation, forcefulness, selective hostility, self-defence, righteous indignation, etc'. He repeatedly attacks the biblical doctrine of original sin. 'If one looks at a healthy and well-loved and cared-for infant ... it is quite impossible to see anything that could be called evil, original sin.'[8] But because we do not understand the causes of psychopathology 'a good many have thrown up their hands altogether and talked about original sin and intrinsic evil and concluded that man could be saved only by extra-human forces.'[9]

Here, then, we see the psychological theories of a man without God. Maslow wants us to believe, contrary to Scripture, that there is no such thing as original sin, and that we can save ourselves from what he labels 'psychopathology'. He even claims that psychotherapy is able to reduce evil.

Hierarchy of needs

Maslow's fundamental theory was that a human being is driven by a set of needs. These needs, he insists, are morally neutral. 'On the surface, the basic needs (motives, impulses, drives) are not evil or sinful ... At our most scientifically cautious, we would still have to say that they are neutral rather than evil ...'[10] In Maslow's view the needs, desires and passions of the human heart are morally neutral. Scripture, however, teaches that we all are tempted when by our own evil desires we are dragged away and enticed. When desire has conceived, it gives birth to sin; and sin, when it is full-grown, brings forth death (James 1.14-15).

Jesus said that from within, out of the human heart come evil thoughts, desires and passions *(Matthew 15.19)*.

Maslow claims that 'there are at least five sets of goals, which we may call basic needs. These are briefly physiological, safety, love, esteem, and self-actualisation.' He argues that for an extremely hungry man, Utopia can be defined very simply as a place where there is plenty of food. If he is guaranteed food for the rest of his life, he will be perfectly happy and never want anything more. 'Life itself tends to be defined in terms of eating. Anything else will be defined as unimportant. Freedom, love, community feeling, respect, philosophy, may all be waved aside as fripperies which are useless since they fail to fill the stomach. Such a man may fairly be said to live by bread alone.'[11]

Maslow's theory directly contradicts the teaching of our Lord who said that man shall not live by bread alone but by every word that proceeds from the mouth of God. We are not to worry about what we will eat or drink, for life is more than food, clothes and security. We are to seek first the kingdom of God and his righteousness and all these things, food, clothes and so on, shall be added, for our heavenly Father knows that we need these things *(Matthew 6)*. We must not labour for the food which perishes, but for the food which endures to everlasting life *(John 6.27)*.

Neurosis a deficiency disease

In response to the question of the origin of neuroses, Maslow explains that at its core, neurosis seems to be a deficiency disease. It is born out of being deprived of certain satisfactions or needs in the same sense that the absence of water, amino acids and calcium produces illness.[12] Maslow argues that a man who is thwarted in any of his basic needs may fairly be seen as a sick man, just as the man who lacks vitamins or minerals. Who is to say that a lack of love is less important than a lack of vitamins? A healthy man is primarily motivated by his needs to develop and actualise his fullest potentialities and capacities. If a man has any other basic needs in any active, chronic sense, then he is simply an unhealthy man.[13]

Here Maslow is propagating the 'man is a victim' syndrome. He cultivates the idea that man is a perpetually 'wanting', thirsty animal. All people have needs that demand to be satisfied. The reason we behave badly is because we have been deprived of certain satisfactions, so it's not our fault. We are a 'victim' of society or of other people who have failed to provide for our needs. There is no recognition that human wants and desires might be evil.

Self-esteem and self-actualisation

Maslow emphasises our need for self-esteem. He claims that all people (with a few pathological exceptions) have a need for a firmly based, high evaluation of themselves. We all need self-esteem and the esteem of others. 'Satisfaction of the self-esteem need leads to feelings of self-confidence, worth, strength, capability and adequacy of being useful and necessary in the world. But thwarting of these needs produces feelings of inferiority, of weakness and of helplessness.'[14] So high self-esteem is a basic human need – if we don't have it we become neurotic. The issue of self-esteem is dealt with in more detail in chapters 12, 13 and 14.

Maslow describes the need for self-actualisation. When all our needs are satisfied, we are still discontented unless we are doing what we are fitted for. 'A musician must make music, an artist must paint, a poet must write, if he is to be ultimately happy. What a man can be, he must be. This need we may call self-actualisation . . . It refers to the desire for self-fulfilment, namely, to the tendency for him to become actualised in what he is potentially. This tendency might be phrased as the desire to become more and more what one is, to become everything that one is capable of becoming.'[15] Scripture, however, teaches that the greatest human need is to be born again of the Spirit of God. It is the Spirit who gives life; the flesh profits nothing. The words of Jesus are spirit, and they are life (John 6.63).

Maslow explains that we only feel the need for self-actualisation when our basic needs for security, safety, love and esteem have been met. 'We shall call people who are satisfied in these needs, basically satisfied people, and it is from these that we may expect the fullest (and healthiest) creativeness. Since, in our society, basically satisfied people are the exception, we do not know much about self-actualisation, either experimentally or clinically.'[16] According to Maslow our physical needs come first, then the higher need of self-actualisation. As we saw above, Jesus teaches exactly the opposite. We are to seek first the kingdom of God and his righteousness, and all these things (physical needs) will be added *(Matthew 6.33)*. Maslow describes peak-experiences, where a self-actualised person has an experience that takes him out of himself, that makes him feel to some extent one with life or nature or a Superior Being. A person feels part of the infinite and the eternal. Peak-experiences tend to change people for the better, and many actively seek them out. They are also called mystical experiences. He claims, 'To the extent that all mystical or peak-experiences are the same in their essence and have always been the same, all religions are the same in their essence and have always been the same.'[17] To Maslow, God is not a person but the integrating principle of the universe.[18] It is not difficult to see that Maslow's peak-experience is similar to the enlightenment experience of Buddhism or New Age.

Self-actualisation, Zen Buddhism and Chinese Taoism

The self-actualisation theories of Abraham Maslow and Carl Rogers (discussed in the next chapter) have had a profound influence on the humanistic psychology movement in the Western world. From a Christian point of view it is important to understand the link between the self-actualisation theories of Maslow and Rogers, and the teachings of Zen Buddhism and Chinese Taoism.

In the paper, 'Characteristics of the self-actualised person: Visions from the East and West', Raylene Chang draws out the similarities. Maslow and Rogers both emphasise that self-actualisation is the optimal psychological condition for all mankind. The aim of psychotherapy is to help people to develop their own potential for self-actualisation. According to Chang, 'Many of the concepts of self-actualisation put forward by Rogers and Maslow are also those that, coincidentally, have been considered elemental in Chinese Taoism and Zen Buddhism.'[19] Both the enlightened person in Zen Buddhism and the sage in Taoism have attained an inner state of perfection, that is, they have developed their human potential to its maximum extent. These belief systems all assume that every person has an actualising tendency that promotes growth, direction and productivity.

Maslow's work has contributed to the development of the transpersonal approach which seeks to blend Eastern religion or Western mysticism with a form of modern psychology. Transpersonal Psychology focuses on spiritual self-development, peak-experiences, mystical experiences, systemic trance and other metaphysical experiences of living.

Salvation through psychotherapy

In Maslow's worldview the problem of man, who is intrinsically good, is that all his needs have not been satisfied. This leads to psychopathology, which is like a deficiency disease. Salvation is through psychotherapy which helps to develop human potential and takes people to the fount of self-actualisation. Maslow asserts that psychotherapists '... every day, as a matter of course, change and improve human nature, help people to become more strong, virtuous, creative, kind, loving, altruistic, serene'.[20]

Maslow does his best to explain away the Christian faith. A critic of Maslow makes the comment: 'Rather than be subject to the demands of God, who has clearly revealed himself in his creation, Maslow denies the supernatural, denies divine revelation, denies authority, and places the would-be autonomous man on the throne.'[21] In Maslow's humanistic philosophy, man is the ultimate reference point, man is the centre of the universe, for in man resides all knowledge and wisdom. It is a philosophy that begins with man and ends with the New Age mysticism of the peak-experience – it is openly hostile to the one true God of the Bible.

Yet Maslow's false psychological worldview that describes man as a wanting, thirsty animal has had a large impact on the Christian counselling movement. We have seen that Larry Crabb bases his theory of sanctification on the psychological model of Abraham Maslow. Selwyn Hughes, no doubt influenced by Maslow, describes a triad of human needs – man as a thirsty being who has deep longings for security (the need to feel loved unconditionally), self-worth (the need to feel valued) and significance (the need for meaning and purpose). Man is at the centre and God's role is to meet the psychological needs of thirsty, needy, wanting humans. This is not the true faith, but a distortion, developed and cultivated by those who have deserted the faith once for all delivered to the saints. The integrationists of the Christian counselling movement must answer this question: 'Has Maslow produced psychological truth that can be placed alongside Scripture?'

8
Carl Rogers – a Man who Believed in Himself

CARL ROGERS is one of the most influential psychologists of the 20th century. A study published in 1982 in the *American Psychologist* journal, five years before Rogers' death, ranked the ten most influential psychotherapists, with Carl Rogers rated as number one. His psychological theories, which incorporate the concept of non-judgementalism, have had a major impact on education policy and psychotherapy. One of his great innovations was to change people seeking psychotherapy from patients into clients. His client-centred, non-directive approach has had a large impact on Christian crisis pregnancy counselling. Larry Crabb recommends that 'Christians would do well to read Carl Rogers on the need for profoundly accepting the client as a worthwhile human being'.[1]

The emphasis on feelings, that is now such a part of Christian counselling, owes much to the psychological approach of Carl Rogers. As Selwyn Hughes points out, 'The more aware we are of our feelings, the sooner we recover from them ... When an emotion arises, don't attempt to deny it or pretend it is not there. Face it and feel it.'[2] Rogers stresses the importance of self-esteem and identifies the human need for positive unconditional self-regard. As a leader of the humanist school of psychology, he sees humans as motivated toward good behaviour. Rogers' scheme is based on the idea of one life-force, a power that he calls the 'actualising tendency'. He believes that this life-force also exists outside the human psyche, for the actualising tendency is present in all forms of life – it is active in the eco-system, in forests and in flowers.[3] It is the same life-force that makes men and women struggle to do good things and create great works of art.

Rogers' move from Christianity to secular humanism

As a young man Carl Rogers entered the liberal Union Theological Seminary and in his junior year went to China for an international World Student Christian Federation Conference. This experience forced him to doubt his parents' Christian worldview, for he felt that he could no longer accept the basic doctrines of the Christian faith. He then went to the Teachers College, Columbia University, where he was strongly influenced by William H. Kilpatrick's courses in the philosophy of education. John Dewey's theory of education, which emphasised experience as the basis for learning, also made a large impact on the young Rogers. Over time he became deeply committed to the cause of secular humanism.

After he finished his studies Rogers worked as a clinical psychologist, specialising in child guidance. It was his experiences with children and their parents that helped him formulate the ideas that would evolve into his person-centred approach. Rogers entered the academic world and worked as a professor at the University of Wisconsin. In 1963 he left academia and until his death in 1987 was a member of independent institutes, first the Western Sciences Behavioural Institute and then the Centre for the Studies of the Person. It was in this period that his writings, especially his book *Freedom to Learn* (1969), began to reflect his broad interests in education and psychology. Such was his commitment to the cause of secular humanism that in 1964 he was elected humanist of the year by the American Humanist Association.

Client-centred, non-directive counselling

Rogers developed an approach to psychotherapy that was person-centred and non-directive. His theory is based on the idea that in every form of life there is an innate motivation to develop as fully as possible. This tendency is known as self-actualisation. Rogers believed that his clients possessed a core self that is essentially healthy. A client has the potential for personal growth in a counselling situation that is non-judgemental, non-directive and empathic. A key objective of non-directive counselling is to help a client uncover and express his true feelings. Rogers found that at an early stage of the counselling process 'there is very little acceptance of feelings. For the most part feelings are revealed as something shameful, bad or abnormal, or unacceptable in other ways.'[4] However, as counselling progresses, 'feelings are very close to being fully experienced'.[5] Rogers wants a client to be free to fully own and express his feelings. A client must be helped to trust his feelings and do what 'feels right' in a particular situation. Yet Rogers' great emphasis on feelings is contrary to the teaching of Scripture. 'A fool vents all his feelings, but a wise man holds them back' *(Proverbs 29.11)*. It is foolishness to think that our feelings will provide a reliable guide to how we should behave.

Throughout the counselling session the client must feel himself as being fully received, just as he is, by the therapist. The attitude and feelings of the therapist are important, for there should be no hint of judgement. The therapist exhibits 'empathic understanding' and fully accepts the client no matter how reprobate his conduct might appear to some people. Rogers wants to help a client to explore himself free from 'any type of moral or diagnostic evaluation, since all such evaluations are, I believe, always threatening'.[6] A client who is compassionately and gently supported by the therapist would discover his own solutions.

Rogers' counselling method is called 'non-directive' because he believed that the counsellor should not lead the client. In successful therapy 'the individual increasingly comes to feel that the locus of evaluation lies within himself. Less and less does he look to others for approval or disapproval; for standards to live by; for decisions and choices. He recognises that it rests within himself to choose.'[7] Rogers believes that the client is the one who should say what is wrong, find ways of improving, and determine the conclusion of therapy.[8] He refers to this non-judgemental caring approach as 'unconditional positive regard'. He stresses the importance of the therapist being genuine with his clients.

Rogers describes four characteristics of the successful therapist. The first is congruence; the good therapist must be able to relate to others with honesty and sincerity. The good therapist must not be defensive when relating to others. Next is empathy – the therapist must be able to put himself in his client's shoes in order to understand the client's feelings and to feel with the client – 'I know what you are feeling.' Third is the ability to learn from the client. The good therapist must be a good listener. Therapy is a two-way street, and the therapist should also benefit from the therapy. The final characteristic is unconditional positive regard. The therapist must genuinely learn to like the client even if he does not approve of his behaviour. He feels his client to be a person of value no matter what his condition, his behaviour or his feelings. He respects him for what he is, and accepts him as he is, with his potentialities.

Experience the source of moral authority

In his book *On Becoming a Person* (1961) Rogers makes it clear that he accepts no authority outside of himself and his experience. He writes, 'Experience is, for me, the highest authority. The touchstone of validity is my own experience. No other person's ideas, and none of my own ideas, are as authoritative as my experience. It is to experience that I must return again and again, to discover a closer approximation to truth as it is in the process of becoming in me.' And lest there be any doubt he goes on, 'Neither the Bible nor the prophets – neither Freud nor research – neither the revelations of God nor man – can take precedence over my own direct experience.' He explains that his 'experience is not authoritative because it is infallible. It is the basis of authority because it can always be checked in new primary ways. In this way its frequent error or fallibility is always open to correction.'[9] The promotion of *self* as the ultimate moral authority is a key objective in Rogerian therapy.

Rogers made it clear that there 'is no philosophy or belief or set of principles which I could encourage or persuade others to have or hold. I can only try to live by my interpretation of the current meaning of my experience, and try to give others the permission and freedom to develop their own inward freedom and thus their own meaningful interpretation of their own experience.'[10] Rogers' view of authority means that he has no objective standard of morality, and therefore no way of judging right and wrong other than his own experience. This view of authority leads to a moral relativism where each person is free to decide his own moral standards. It follows that if something feels right, it probably is. In Rogers' worldview there is no place for the moral law of God, and no place for moral absolutes. Having rejected the Christian faith, he has no moral compass by which to live; no source of wisdom or truth on which to base his life. As a moral relativist, his mission was to destroy belief in any moral system that judged certain forms of human behaviour as right or wrong. Rogers taught that we must be non-judgemental and free to decide our own version of right and wrong.

The inherent goodness of man

Rogers believes in the innate tendency of human beings to make good choices. In a speech delivered to students at a Midwest college he said, 'The basic nature of the human being, when functioning freely is constructive and trustworthy. For me this is an inescapable conclusion from a quarter-century of psychotherapy.'[11]

Rogers rejects the biblical view of man as fallen and sinful. He is upset that the Christian faith teaches the doctrine of original sin. 'Religion, especially the Protestant Christian tradition, has permeated our culture with the concept that man is basically sinful, and only by something approaching a miracle can his sinful nature be negated.'[12] He saw human nature as inherently good, moving in a positive direction. Beneath the inner hurt is a self that is positive and without hate. There is within us all the capacity and tendency to move forward toward maturity.[13] However, this tendency may be deeply buried under layer after layer of psychological defences. The purpose of counselling is to help a client to do what feels right, for this 'proves to be a competent and trustworthy guide to behaviour which is truly satisfying'.[14]

Positive self-regard or self-esteem

Rogers believes that self-esteem, or what he calls 'positive self-regard', is essential for psychological health. We achieve healthy self-esteem by experiencing positive regard from others while we are growing up. Without this positive self-regard, we feel small, insignificant and help-less. Lack of self-esteem hinders our psychological growth. For the vast majority of people who do not have an optimal childhood their best hope to develop toward psychological maturity is through therapy.

Unconditional positive regard

According to Rogers we can only develop optimally if we experience 'unconditional positive regard'. The idea of *unconditional* positive regard is really a forerunner of the idea of unconditional love. Rogers teaches that psychological growth requires that a child feels that he is being valued and loved regardless of the degree to which his behaviours are approved or disapproved. *Conditional* positive regard, on the other hand, is the granting of love and approval only when a child behaves in accordance with his parents' wishes. It leads to conditions of worth which, in turn, lead to alienation from true feelings, and anxiety which blocks psychological growth.

Self-actualisation

Carl Rogers' person-centred theory emphasises the concept of 'self-actualisation'. This concept implies that within all people is an internal, biological force to develop human capacities and talents to the fullest. *Unconditional* positive regard is necessary to achieve self-actualisation. Growth occurs when we confront problems, struggle to master them, and through that struggle develop new skills, capacities and views about life. Life, therefore, is an endless process of creatively moving forward, even if only in small ways. Rogers uses the term 'fully functioning person' for someone who is self-actualising. These people are open to experiencing their feelings, and their lives are full of meaning, challenge and fulfilment. Rogers believes that we all have within ourselves the capacity, even if latent, to move forward toward self-actualisation. In a suitable psychological climate this tendency is released and becomes actual rather than potential.

The legacy of Rogers

The legacy of Rogers' non-judgemental, non-directive ideology can be found in the school classroom and the abortion counselling office. William Kilpatrick, professor in moral education and adolescent psychology, explains the influence of Carl Rogers' approach. 'In the 1940s and 50s Carl Rogers and others had pioneered a method of counselling that was non-directive, non-judgemental, and client-centred. Have you heard this name, Carl Rogers? Along with Abraham Maslow, he was one of the founding fathers of what became known as humanistic psychology or human potential psychology. Rogers is not the best known of psychologists but I don't think any other psychologist has had as much influence on our culture and ways of thinking. In the 60s and 70s these counselling techniques which Rogers had developed were introduced into schools with the result that teachers began to take a non-directive, non-judgemental attitude toward values. Each person would have to discover his own values, and no one could say that one value was superior to another.'[15]

The consequences of Rogers' non-judgemental philosophy have been catastrophic for the moral education of children. Why can't Johnny tell right from wrong? Kilpatrick explains, 'Because we're not teaching him the difference between the two. Because we're relying instead on an experimental approach – an experiment in having children construct their own morality.'[16]

Non-directive abortion counselling

Virtually all abortion counselling services, both Christian and secular, follow Rogers' non-directive approach. The aim is to provide a pregnant woman with the facts about her options (abortion, adoption, keeping the pregnancy) in an impartial way that helps her to make up her mind as to what she wants to do with the unwanted pregnancy. Whatever choice she makes is the right choice for her. Rogers' counselling method was called 'non-directive' because he believed that the woman should make her own decision about what she wants, free from outside influences or advice.

A pro-choice organisation, the Allan Guttmacher Institute, produced a report outlining professional standards for pregnancy counsellors in the USA which was based on Rogers' non-directive model of counselling. Abortion counsellors must provide *neutral*, factual information and *non-directive counselling* on each of the options. The Department of Health and Human Services points out that 'non-directive' means that counsellors '*may not steer or direct clients* toward selecting any option'.[17]

In the UK the Christian crisis pregnancy counselling scene is deeply committed to Rogers' non-directive model. Christian Action, Research and Education (CARE), a well established mainstream Christian charity, has a network of crisis pregnancy centres scattered around the UK. CARE explains that its counsellors are trained in non-directional counselling to help a pregnant woman find out how she feels about having an abortion. A client must be helped to trust her feelings and do what 'feels right' in a particular situation. Consistent with Rogers' non-directive model, CARE's leaflet *Making a Decision* uses the words 'feel' or 'feelings' twenty-three times. 'Having looked at all the facts and explored thoroughly how you feel about each option, you may be ready to make your decision. It's important that you feel able to live with the decision you have made.' According to the CARE Centres Network website: 'Pregnancy counselling centres are there to help you find out how you *feel* about having an abortion.' Here we should note that while CARE claims to be a Christian organisation, its non-directive counselling, based on the philosophy of Carl Rogers, is in direct opposition to the teaching of Scripture.

LIFE is another pro-life organisation in the UK that is proud to use Rogers' non-directive model of counselling to help pregnant mothers who may be considering an abortion. LIFE believes that counsellors should be non-judgemental and provide an empathic understanding. LIFE's non-directive, non-judgemental approach is built on the idea that no woman actually wants an abortion, and that people are intrinsically good and naturally seek right from wrong.[18]

A world of spiritual darkness

In *A Way of Being* (1980), published towards the end of his life, Rogers describes his growing involvement with the occult. He became interested in new ideas that have to do with inner space. 'I am open to even more mysterious phenomena – precognition, thought transference, clairvoyance, human auras, Kirlian photography, even out-of-the-body experiences.'[19]

Rogers and his wife Helen, shortly before her death, attended a séance in which, with the help of a medium, they spoke with her deceased sister. Just before she died 'Helen had a vision of an inspiring white light which came close, lifted her from the bed, and then deposited her back on the bed.'[20] Rogers describes various visions that his wife had just before she died. 'Yet, upon invitation, she and I visited a thoroughly honest medium, who would take no money. There, Helen experienced, and I observed, a "contact" with her deceased sister, involving facts that the medium could not possibly have known. The messages were extraordinarily convincing, and all came through the tipping of a sturdy table, tapping out letters. Later, when the medium came to our home and *my own table* tapped out messages in our living room, I could only be open to an incredible, and certainly non-fraudulent, experience.'[21] (Italics in the original.)

After Helen's death Rogers again consulted the medium and claims to have called up his recently departed wife to hear about her experience of 'the white light and spirits coming for her'.[22]

Here then is the story of Carl Rogers, the man whose counselling theories have had a massive influence on Western thought and have been readily embraced by the Christian counselling movement. His humanist worldview proved so inadequate that at the end of his life he turned to the occult for comfort. It seems he felt unable to deal with death and the judgement to come.

Rogers' central idea was the glorification of self. He rejected all ideas of a moral authority that lay outside of man. To him we are all free to develop our own morality, to decide for ourselves what is right and wrong. His non-directive, non-judgemental counselling aims to remove the annoying concepts of guilt and sin from the human condition, but it does so at the cost of either denying evil altogether or attributing responsibility for it entirely to others. The purpose of his client-centred therapy is to make us feel good about our selfishness and sin. So the woman who undergoes non-directive counselling can abort her unborn baby without feeling guilty. Everything revolves around me, my feelings and my satisfaction – getting my way, doing what I want. Sinful man becomes the source of his own morality and sets his own standards, for there is no higher authority, there is no God to whom he is accountable.

Yet, in the ultimate analysis, Carl Rogers has nothing to contribute to a Christian view of sanctification, for he did not realise that the 'way that seems right to man' is the way that ends in death *(Proverbs 14.12)*.

9
Albert Ellis – the Aggressive Atheist

ALBERT ELLIS (1913-2007) is the psychologist who developed Rational Emotive Behaviour Therapy (REBT). He is considered by many to be the grandfather of cognitive-behavioural therapies and, based on a study published in 1982 in the *American Psychologist*, the second most influential psychotherapist in history, after Carl Rogers. The survey rated Freud third. As a reward for his forthright promotion of non-theistic humanism, in 1971 he was recognised as Humanist of the Year.

The assumption behind REBT is that our emotional reactions are largely caused by our conscious and unconscious beliefs and philosophies. The Albert Ellis Institute describes REBT as a practical approach to coping with problems and enhancing personal growth. It focuses on attitudes, emotions and behaviours that sabotage a fuller experience of life and helps develop a philosophy of living that enhances the client's emotional health and personal welfare.[1] REBT practitioners seek to uncover beliefs (attitudes, expectations and personal rules) that lead to emotional distress and then provide a variety of methods to help people change their faulty beliefs into more sensible, realistic and helpful ones.

The therapist uses the so-called ABC theory of behaviour to

demonstrate the link between behaviours, beliefs and emotions and to show how irrational beliefs inevitably lead to problems. A is for activating experiences, such as family troubles, unsatisfying work, early childhood traumas, and the many things that are the sources of our unhappiness. B stands for beliefs, especially the irrational, self-defeating beliefs that are the actual sources of our unhappiness. C is for consequences that come from our beliefs – neurotic symptoms and negative emotions such as depression, panic, and rage.

Selwyn Hughes and the ABC theory of behaviour

Selwyn Hughes, in his book *Christ Empowered Living*, provides an explanation of Ellis' ABC theory of behaviour. 'Just as when reading the alphabet you do not go from A to C without passing through B, so the theory says that any event or circumstance (A) is powerless in itself to produce an emotional response (C) until it has been evaluated. In other words, A does not produce C; it has to pass through B.'[2] Hughes confesses, 'I have no difficulty with the ABC theory of behaviour, and I have often used it when counselling.'[3]

The Crusade for World Evangelism (CWR) uses Albert Ellis' theory to help people suffering with eating disorders. The book *Insight into Eating Disorders* (2006), published by CWR, explains that 'the thinking behind an eating disorder controls the future happiness, freedom and potential of the individual. It is essential for thinking to change in order for recovery from an eating disorder.'[4] The reader is advised that the ABC theory of behaviour is the pathway to recovery, for it is essential for the sufferer to work on her faulty belief system. 'Faulty thinking arises out of messages received as a child which are further developed and distorted as an adult . . . Albert Ellis and his colleagues identified ten common irrational beliefs which, if held too rigidly, are likely to lead to emotional distress. These beliefs are learned early in life and become the bedrock from which our thinking patterns spring.'[5] One particular error, identified by ABC, is to think in absolutes, as black or white, good or bad, with no middle ground.[6] Another irrational belief is to live by fixed rules and regularly use the words 'should', 'ought', 'must' and 'can't'. 'This leads to unnecessary guilt and disappointment. The more rigid these statements are the more disappointed, angry, depressed or guilty you are likely to feel.'[7] So women receive counsel from CWR that rigid, fixed rules are the underlying cause of their emotional problems. Here we should note that the Ten Commandments are rigid, fixed rules which use the term 'you shall not' nine times. The counselling given to women with eating disorders by CWR is firmly based in the wisdom of Albert Ellis.

Ellis' early career

The most dominant influence in Albert Ellis' life was his public embrace of atheism. In an interview he declared, 'I became an atheist at 12 and still think, in all probability [voice rising], that there is no God, just as there is no Santa Claus, fairies, or angels. I found out in sixth grade that the world was created in billions of years of evolution. That knocked off my Sunday-school view that the world was created in seven days.' Asked what he thought happened after death Ellis continued, 'Zero. That's what I teach my clients. It's exactly the same state you were in before you were conceived. Zero. No pain, no joy, zero. So you better go and have a [expletive] ball in this life.'[8]

As a young man Ellis studied business at the City University of New York. After a brief career in business, he tried his hand at writing, but had no success in publishing his fiction. He then turned his hand to research and writing on human sexuality. He wrote widely on the subject, including a treatise called 'The Case for Sexual Liberty'. His experience as a sexual counsellor convinced him to study clinical psychology at Columbia University, where he was trained in psychoanalysis.

But he had serious philosophical objections to psychoanalysis, which he thought was too passive and not very effective. And so he took a more active role as a counsellor, interjecting advice as he had done when he was counselling people with sexual problems. He concentrated on changing people's behaviour by confronting them with their irrational beliefs and persuading them to adopt rational ones. He believed that his clients improved more quickly than when he used a passive psychoanalytic approach.

In the early 1950s Ellis began to propagate his new technique and in 1957 he formally announced cognitive behaviour therapy as the treatment for neuroses. In *How to Live with a Neurotic* (1957) he explained his new method. He wrote over 60 books and numerous articles on

REBT, sex and marriage. Within a few decades REBT had become main-stream in the world of counselling.

The hedonistic worldview of Albert Ellis

Albert Ellis was an unabashed hedonist, humanist and atheist. Writing in *Is Objectivism a Religion* (1968), Ellis asserts that 'morality is normally based on the philosophy of enlightened self-interest ... if we want to define morality as first, taking care of ourselves and second, avoiding needless harm to others, and never damning them totally (giving them unconditional acceptance), that seems fine.'[9]

Ellis states in his published works that REBT is based on the moral philosophy of hedonism. In *Reason and Emotion in Psychotherapy* (1962) he writes: 'Just about all existing schools of psychotherapy are, at bottom hedonistic, in that they hold that pleasure and freedom from pain are good and preferably should be the aims of thought and action. This is probably inevitable, because people who do not believe in a hedonistic view would continue to suffer intense anxiety and discomfort and would not come for therapy. And therapists who did not try in some manner to alleviate the discomfort of those who did come for help would hardly remain in business very long. Rational Emotive Behaviour therapists, therefore, are far from unique when they accept some kind of a hedonistic worldview and try to help clients work for a hedonistic way of life.'[10]

Hatred of true Christianity

While Ellis regarded all religion as mere 'supernatural nonsense', he had a deep aversion that bordered on the pathological for what he called 'fanatical religionists'. He believed that religious people, motivated by their own worthlessness, have invented a God or gods. He frequently uses the term 'fanatical religionists' to describe Bible-believing Christians, against whom he directs his greatest venom. 'Fanatic religionists believe strongly in some kind of faith unfounded on fact, and frequently believe in spite of observable facts that contradict their belief system. They tend to be highly unscientific, unrealistic, anti-empirical, romantic, and utopian. They frequently make up or believe in myths and fairy tales; and stubbornly refuse to accept certain aspects of reality that oppose their religion.'[11]

What Ellis cannot stand about religion is its moral teaching – he simply hates the idea of good and evil, of sin, of guilt. He would do away with all that. As a humanist he believes that every human being has value, and therefore no human should be seen as fundamentally bad.

In *The Case against Religion* Ellis argues that 'if religion is defined as man's dependence on a power above and beyond the human, then, as a psychotherapist, I find it to be exceptionally pernicious.'[12] All true believers 'are distinctly disturbed, since they are obviously rigid, fanatic and dependent individuals'.[13] Ellis makes the point that 'unbelief, scepticism, and thoroughgoing atheism not only abet but are practically synonymous with mental health; and that devout belief, dogmatism, and religiosity distinctly contribute to and in some ways are equal to mental or emotional disturbance'.[14]

According to Ellis 'the facts of history tend to show that the existence of a Jehovah-like God is improbable'.[15] Moreover, reliance on the Almighty has distinct emotional dangers. So 'instead of striving to be dependent on other individuals (or on some hypothetical Higher Power) you can try to stand on your own two feet and to do your own thinking and acting . . . '[16]

Ellis goes so far as to say that relying on God 'may well become an obsessive-compulsive disturbance in its own right and lead to immense harm to other people and to oneself'.[17] It follows that the REBT therapist cannot simply accept his patient's religious beliefs – they must be attacked and eradicated.[18]

Ellis concluded his case against religion with these words. 'In the final analysis, then, religion is neurosis . . . If the thesis of this article is correct, religion goes hand in hand with the basic irrational beliefs of human beings. These keep them dependent, anxious, and hostile, and thereby create and maintain their neuroses and psychoses. What then is the role of psychotherapy in dealing with the religious views of disturbed patients? Obviously, the sane and effective psychotherapist should not . . . go along with the patients' religious orientation and try to help these patients live successfully with their religions, for this is equivalent to trying to help them live successfully with their emotional illness.'[19]

Absolute truth, absolute morality

In an interview before an audience of psychotherapists, Ellis objected to the use of the word absolute. 'Don't use "absolutely". That's a human sickness. There are no absolutes . . . I do what I like and I do what I dislike, but I never get into trouble. I'm a long-range hedonist . . . and go after what I want. But if I don't get it, that's too bad.'[20]

At the centre of Ellis' thinking is the rejection of absolute truth and absolute moral standards. Most neurotic feelings, according to Ellis, are accompanied by the demands of moral absolutes. In other words, God's moral law is the underlying cause of neurosis. REBT is also fundamentally opposed to absolute truth. Ellis explains that REBT agrees with the postmodernists that there is no objective standpoint from which to judge whether something is an absolute truth.[21] And he stresses this point, 'As far as we can tell, there is no certainty, perfection, nor absolute truth in the world . . . we live in a world of probability and chance, and we can be certain of nothing external to ourselves.'[22]

In particular, Ellis has a strong aversion to the concept of absolute right and wrong. He despises committed Christians who strive to live by the teachings of Scripture. 'Fanatical religionists believe in absolutes: in unqualified and unconditional creeds. They have a desperate need for certainty, and essentially strive to be perfect and infallible. They are anxious about doing the wrong thing . . . As a part of their absolutism, they frequently believe in some superhuman or infallible God, who will completely be on their side and who will help them to be angelic.'[23] True, Christians do believe the absolute truth that there is one true God, who has revealed himself to mankind through his eternal, unchanging Word and through Jesus Christ, his only Son.

To Ellis the idea that humans should be held accountable for their actions is nonsense. 'Many true believers are condemning and punitive toward other people who display "erroneous" or "wrong" behaviour. They not only have powerful, dogmatic moral codes of behaviour; but they moralistically believe that everyone should follow these codes and that they should be condemned, and perhaps roasted everlastingly in some kind of hell, if they do not.'[24] Again true, Christians do believe in the absolute moral law of God and that all people will stand before the judgement throne of God.

Ellis claims that 'it is often wise to compromise between truth and falsehood and between reason and irrationality. For there are no absolute standards of truth and reason – at least, none that has yet been established to the satisfaction of all philosophers and scientists.'[25]

For Ellis there is no such thing as sexual immorality. 'As for sexual desire devoid of love being depravity – shades of nineteenth-century Puritanism! To virtually any self-accepting contemporary individual, sex is good in, of, by, and for itself. It may often be better, or more enjoyable, when it is experienced in the context of a loving human relationship. But loveless sex is not in the least depraved – except by arbitrary, puritanical definitions.'[26] Ellis has a permissive view of sin and wrongdoing. He believes that individuals can be wrong, mistaken, irresponsible, and can even choose to be wrongdoers, but can nonetheless accept themselves, not be condemned as people and not deserve to be punished for their irresponsibility.

Unconditional self-acceptance

REBT promotes the idea of unconditional self-acceptance. Ellis consistently attacks the 'irrational' belief that many people are bad, wicked or villainous and that they should be severely blamed and punished for their sins. He makes his aversion to the concept of sin clear. We should not use words like 'sin' and 'sinner' because they imply absolute, God-given standards that condemn us for some of our mistaken acts.[27] Although people have strong tendencies to judge themselves, they act irrationally when they do so. Self-evaluation leads to depression and repression, and avoidance of change. The best thing for human health is that we should stop evaluating ourselves altogether. Here Ellis is acknowledging that the self-evaluation of our conscience leads to feelings of depression. One of the aims of REBT is to silence our conscience.

It follows that REBT does not accept any form of judgement, and therefore no one should be condemned or damned, no matter how awful their actions. We should learn to accept ourselves for what we are rather than for what we have achieved. Human beings have value just for being alive.

A remarkable U-turn

Late in life Albert Ellis had a Damascus road experience. When he came to understand that the vast majority of people are religious and believe in God, and when he realised that many skilled REBT practitioners are religious, including a host of Christian counsellors and some ordained ministers, his eyes were opened to see that not all religions are that bad. In a remarkable U-turn, Ellis confesses that he has changed his mind about religion. He is not against all religion – only against true biblical Christianity. 'I also once believed that religion itself was largely harmful to humans, because it has many dangers and limitations. But I later realised that there are many different kinds of religion and that some were partly beneficial, and some were rarely so. I therefore published a paper showing that religiosity rather than religion was dangerous to mental health and happy living. By religiosity, I meant devout, absolutistic, fanatical religion.'[28] The absolute religion that Ellis has in mind is, of course, biblical Christianity.

In order to attract Christian counsellors into the REBT fold, Ellis has been careful to state that his therapy is independent of his atheism, even admitting that belief in a loving God is probably psychologically healthy. Such has been his change of heart, that he has co-authored the book *Counselling and Psychotherapy with Religious Persons: A Rational Emotive Behaviour Approach* (2001), which claims that REBT 'is uniquely and exceptionally well suited to treating the problems and concerns of religious clients . . . it discusses why interventions derived from the theory of REBT are seldom at odds with clients' religious beliefs even when the client and therapist have very different religious orientations – even when a devoutly religious client, for example, is treated by a nonreligious, atheistic therapist.'[29]

So how do we explain this remarkable turnaround? It seems that when Ellis realised that Christian counsellors were actually using his REBT, he came to the amazing realisation that the Christian counselling movement was, in fact, his ally. It was the devout, absolutist Christians who were the enemy. Moreover, as most people in Western society were nominal Christians, there was potentially a large market for REBT, and Ellis was not going to let his atheism stand in the way. So not all religions were as bad as he originally thought, only the religion of Bible-believing, absolutist Christians!

Christian counselling

There is no doubt that the counselling system developed by Albert Ellis is aggressively against the God of the Bible. The basic presupposition is that God's absolute moral law is the cause of mankind's emotional problems. REBT promotes a permissive and hedonistic way of life by excusing sinful behaviour and encouraging self-justification. It avoids the reality of sin and is blind to its consequences.

Here we must pose the question. How can the Christian counselling movement accept a psychological model that is fundamentally opposed to God's Word? Yet the blindness of the Christian counselling movement is such that it is perfectly happy to integrate the ideas of Albert Ellis into its counselling armoury. The fact that the whole system is hostile to the Christian faith seems to make no difference.

The legacy of Albert Ellis

So what kind of man was the founder of REBT? One of his proudest claims is that he was the first psychologist ever to use four-letter expletives at the American Psychological Association conference. According to a news report: 'The attendees of his Friday workshops who get picked to undergo one-on-one REBT demonstrations in front of the crowd occasionally feel more like victims than patients during his expletive-laden sessions.'

But all has not been happiness and light in the citadel of REBT. The trustees of the Albert Ellis Institute removed its founder from his professional duties and from the board of his own Institute. It appears that Ellis could be a very difficult and opinionated man – when crossed in a board meeting he was known to erupt in obscenities. Things came to a head in 2005 when there was a bitter dispute over the management policies of the Institute, and in particular, over the amount of money the Institute was asked to pay for Albert's medical bills. Just before his death he was bringing civil court actions against those who had removed him. His reinstatement was being championed by the Justice for Albert Ellis Campaign. Ellis expressed his bitterness against the Institute's new director when responding to a question on how to deal with a control freak. Ellis reportedly said: 'You *should* be able to kill them, but there are laws against that. That's what Michael Broder is – the director of this institute. He's a power freak! And it would be better if he were dead, dead, dead!'[30] Albert Ellis, it seems, was in need of REBT. He died aged 93 in July 2007.

10

The Bible's Verdict on Psychological 'Truth'

OVER THE PREVIOUS FIVE CHAPTERS we have glimpsed the worldly wisdom of five giants from the world of psychotherapy. We have seen that Sigmund Freud, the man who invented the unconscious, had an unnatural interest in the occult and an intense hatred of the Christian faith. Alfred Adler was a humanist who supported the godless philosophy of Nietzsche. Abraham Maslow was hostile to the Gospel and his peak-experiences involved New Age thinking. Carl Rogers, a man who rejected all moral authority other than his own experience, at the end of his life engaged in necromancy. Albert Ellis was an arrogant, foul-mouthed hedonist devoid of morality who despised devout Christians, referring to them as 'fanatical religionists'. The common ground between these five men is that they were secular humanists who, in their lives and theories, rejected the God of Scripture. They are the foundation and pillars of 'psychological truth'. It is the psychological speculation that has come from the minds of these godless men that the Christian counselling movement is integrating into the church of Jesus Christ.

The giants of psychotherapy, in their voluminous writings, have made it absolutely clear that they reject the wisdom of Scripture. Thus the house of Christian counselling has been built on the sand of human wisdom, on the ideas and theories of men who gloried in their godlessness.

Freud's great contribution to psychological 'truth' is the notion that the unconscious mind is the driving force behind human behaviour. We are all victims of our unconscious, for we are driven by motives, impulses and desires of which we are unaware and over which we have no control. Only a psychotherapist can unlock the unconscious and provide release from its bondage.

We have heard Carl Rogers boast that his own experience was for him the highest moral authority. 'Neither the Bible nor the prophets – neither Freud nor research – neither the revelations of God nor man – can take precedence over my own direct experience.' We have heard Abraham Maslow's staggering claim that his psychology, not Scripture, can produce a system of moral absolutes. In his arrogance, he declared that if his assumptions about human nature are true, 'they promise a scientific ethic, a natural value system, a court of ultimate appeal for the determination of good and bad, of right and wrong. The more we learn about man's natural tendencies, the easier it will be to tell him how to be good, how to be happy, how to be fruitful, how to respect himself, how to love, how to fulfil his highest potentialities.'[1]

We have heard Albert Ellis argue that 'if religion is defined as man's dependence on a power above and beyond the human, then, as a psychotherapist, I find it to be exceptionally pernicious.'[2] All true believers 'are distinctly disturbed, since they are obviously rigid, fanatic and dependent individuals'.[3] Ellis had the effrontery to claim that a true faith in Christ is a form of mental illness. In his folly, Ellis declared that the therapist should not go along with their clients' religious orientation, 'for this is equivalent to trying to help them live successfully with their emotional illness'.[4] The task of the therapist is to eradicate their clients' Christian faith.

Alfred Adler, while more circumspect in his opposition to the God of the Bible, was a committed humanist who was strongly influenced by the ideas of Nietzsche. His idea that our behaviour is controlled by a 'fictional' life goal, of which we are unaware, is highly deterministic and denies the power of God's Word.

The giants of psychology disregard the spiritual dimension of life, deny the doctrine of original sin, and reject the moral law of God. It is not difficult to see that the psychological speculations of these men are *fundamentally* opposed to the most basic doctrines of the Christian faith. Scripture teaches that the problem of human behaviour lies in the heart of man – out of the heart comes all manner of sinful conduct, from sexual immorality, to deceit, theft, covetousness, pride and murder. 'For all have sinned and fall short of the glory of God' *(Romans 3.23)*. Why have the giants of psychology got it so wrong? With all their vast learning, deep knowledge of human nature and multitude of books and scientific papers, why can they not see that the cause of human problems lies in the heart of man? To answer these questions we need to turn to God's Word. We have heard the wisdom of the giants of psychology, now we must listen to the wisdom from above – it is time for the Bible to speak.

The foolishness of secular psychology

Wisdom literature has a great deal to say about human foolishness. The basic principle is this: 'The fear of the Lord is the beginning of knowledge, but fools despise wisdom and instruction' *(Proverbs 1.7)*. Jesus said that the wise man builds his house on the rock of God's Word, whereas the foolish man builds his house on the sand of his own ideas. Scripture warns that a man should not lean on his own understanding: 'Do not be wise in your own eyes; fear the Lord and depart from evil' *(Proverbs 3.7)*. The man who says in his heart, 'There is no God', is a fool *(Psalm 53.1)*. The reason the giants of psychology have got it so wrong is that they are fools with darkened minds *(Romans 1.21)*.

The key characteristic of the fool is that he is wise in his own eyes and lacks moral character, for 'fools mock at sin' *(Proverbs 14.9)*. The fool rejects true wisdom and trusts in his own heart *(Proverbs 28.26)*. When Carl Rogers said that he rejected all authority but his own experience he was showing himself to be a fool.

Another characteristic of the fool is that he blurts out folly *(Proverbs 12.23)* and finds pleasure in his evil conduct. 'To do evil is like sport to a fool' *(Proverbs 10.23)*. Albert Ellis, by his intemperate, unreasonable and outspoken attacks on God's absolute moral law, was showing himself to be a fool. The fool loves talking and hearing his own voice. 'But the lips of a fool shall swallow him up; the words of his mouth begin with foolishness, and the end of his talk is raving madness. A fool also multiplies words' *(Ecclesiastes 10.12-14)*. Freud's voluminous writings, his ridiculous speculations about an Oedipus complex are the rambling thoughts of a foolish mind. It is significant that the giants of psychology have produced many books – there seems to be no end to their foolish words, for 'the mouth of fools pours forth foolishness' *(Proverbs 15.2)*.

The apostle Paul explains the spiritual darkness of those, like the giants of psychology, who suppress the truth about God by their godlessness and wickedness. Those who deny God become futile in their thinking and their foolish hearts are darkened *(Romans 1.18, 21)*. Scripture declares the worldly wisdom of Freud, Adler, Maslow, Rogers and Ellis to be foolish in the eyes of God *(1 Corinthians 1.20)*. These men are scoffing fools who have denied their Creator. They have rejected the most fundamental truth of all, that God has created a moral universe and that man is morally accountable to his Creator. Their blinded minds do not want to understand that mankind has rebelled against God and that all men, including the giants of psychology, are slaves to sin. The giants of psychology understand nothing of the consequences of sin – they do not acknowledge that the wages of sin is death. They do not know that God is not mocked, that a man reaps what he sows. They do not accept that all people, including the giants of psychology, face the judgement of God. It follows, as night follows day, that the giants of psychology have no true understanding of the human condition. Professing to be wise, they have shown themselves to be fools *(Romans 1.22)*.

Is it possible that these men, with their darkened minds and foolish theories, can have anything important to say about solving human problems? No, for their psychological theories of human behaviour are devoid of truth. Their advice on how to solve human problems is no more than the meaningless ravings of futile, darkened minds.

But there is something even more disturbing, for the giants of psychotherapy are scoffers who have set themselves against the God of the Bible and his Anointed One. They are enemies of the Gospel of

Christ. When the Bible speaks of men of perverted speech who forsake the paths of uprightness to walk in the ways of darkness, who rejoice in doing evil and delight in the perverseness of evil, men whose ways are crooked and who are devious in their paths *(Proverbs 2.12-15)*, it speaks of Freud, Adler, Maslow, Rogers and Ellis, scoffing fools who delight in evil.

Integrating psychological and biblical truth?

In chapter 4 we heard the argument of the integrationists who seek to integrate the truth that comes from biblical revelation with psychological truth into a unified view of 'all truth'. This unified view of truth is supposed to help us understand human nature and show us how to solve human problems. The difficulty with the 'unity of truth' doctrine is that it does not recognise the fundamental difference between God's revealed truth and the 'wisdom' of the world that comes from flawed human reason. The 'psychological truth' that comes from Freud, Adler, Maslow, Rogers and Ellis, is little more than the ramblings of depraved minds. Having rejected God, they became futile in their thoughts, and their foolish hearts were darkened. Although they profess to be wise, they are condemned by Scripture as ungodly men who suppress the truth of God in unrighteousness *(Romans 1.18)*. To integrate their foolishness with Scripture is anathema.

Jesus promised to send the Spirit of Truth to guide his followers into all truth *(John 16.13)*. He made it clear that the world cannot receive the Spirit of Truth, for only the disciples of Jesus are indwelt by the Holy Spirit of Truth. An essential work of the Spirit of Truth is to convict the world of sin, and of righteousness and of judgement *(John 16.8)*. Psychological 'truth', however, stands in direct opposition to the Spirit of Truth, for it denies the existence of sin, righteousness and judgement as it seeks to make people feel good in their sin and unrighteousness.

When Jesus appeared before Pilate he said, 'For this cause I was born, and for this cause I have come into the world, that I should bear witness to the truth. *Everyone who is of the truth hears My voice*' *(John 18.37)*. All who love the truth listen to the words of Christ. But the giants of secular psychology have refused to hear the voice of Christ because they do not love God's truth. They have refused to come into the light of the Gospel of Christ. 'And this is the condemnation, that the light has come into the world, and men loved darkness rather than light, because their deeds were evil. For everyone practising evil hates the light and does not come to the light, lest his deeds should be exposed' *(John 3.19-20).*

Opposed to the truth of God is the devil, who was a liar from the beginning. Jesus said, 'He ... does not stand in the truth, because there is no truth in him. When he speaks a lie, he speaks from his own resources, for he is a liar and the father of it [lies]' *(John 8.44).* The devil and his followers hate the truth. Because the world is controlled by a spirit of deception, Christians are warned not to believe every spirit, but to test the spirits, for there are many false prophets in the world. The giants of psychology are of the world, and the world eagerly receives their foolish messages. Christians are warned 'beware lest anyone cheat you through philosophy and empty deceit, according to the basic principles of the world, and not according to Christ' *(Colossians 2.8).*

The apostle Paul outlines an important biblical principle that will help us to make a valid assessment of the giants of psychology. According to Scripture godless men are deceived by their sin, their thoughts are futile and their understanding darkened, being separated from the life of God because of the ignorance that is in them *(Ephesians 4.18).* The giants of psychology, who separated themselves from the life of God, were ignorant men with hearts darkened by sin. Their psychological theories are the product of futile minds and darkened hearts – foolishness in God's sight and worthless. Scripture warns that 'the counsels of the wicked are deceitful' *(Proverbs 12.5).* Can worldly psychology lead the church into yet more truth? No, for the Spirit of Truth 'will guide you into *all* truth' *(John 16.13).*

The Bible is not enough

Another argument of the integrationists is that as the Bible is not a text book of psychology it does not comment on common psychological problems. Integrationists argue that the Bible is good and well as far as it goes, but it is just not enough, for it does not deal adequately with the deep, complex issues people face today. Just as Christians use the truths that emerge from medical practice to treat diseases of the body, so it is perfectly in order for Christians to use psychological truths to treat disorders of the mind. Integrationists claim that the theories of Freud and Adler, and more recently of psychologists such as Rogers, Maslow and Albert Ellis provide appealing explanations of human behaviour and offer useful advice for helping people. The church benefits from the insights of psychology, for the Bible does not have the answers to all our deep-seated psychological problems. We have seen David Seamands claim that many sincere, Spirit-filled Christians have profound problems from which they need deliverance and no amount of advice, no amount of Scripture or prayer can bring them lasting deliverance.[5] Prayer, repentance, being filled with the Holy Spirit, and other biblical remedies are not enough because some psychological problems require something more. We have heard Kirsten Birkett argue that if our minds are not working properly – if our knowledge is not filtering through correctly to the rest of our beliefs – then our mind needs treatment, regardless of how much we 'know' about the Gospel.

So we need psychological theories to help us understand the profound problems that the Bible does not deal with. It simply makes sense to use the remedies that are widely available for helping hurting people. We need more than the Bible has to offer. Ruth Graham McIntire, daughter of Billy Graham, upon learning of her husband's five-year affair testifies: 'I became depressed. I realised I needed professional help. This wasn't easy for me to admit. In my growing up years, it was implied that God and the Bible were all I needed – and resorting to a psychologist meant that you have "spiritual problems". Despite feeling terribly inadequate and continuing to fear that others would find out, I sought professional counselling.'[6] Here is a testimony of someone who felt that 'God and the Bible' were not enough to help with her marital problems. She believed that her psychologist offered the 'more' that God and the Bible could not provide.

The fallacy of this argument is that it is based on the idea that the Scripture is not sufficient for dealing with profound behavioural problems. Yet the Bible declares that God has given to the believer 'all things that pertain to life and godliness' (2 Peter 1.3). And God has blessed Christians 'with every spiritual blessing in the heavenly places in Christ' (Ephesians 1.3). Christians do not need the wisdom of the world that flows from secular psychology. We don't need help from Freud and his friends to live a life worthy of the Gospel.

The argument of the integrationist that biblical truth and psychological theories have equal claim upon our understanding of human problems is seriously flawed. The assertion that Christians need more than the Bible offers for facing the problems of daily living is contrary to Scripture.

God's common grace

In chapter 4 we saw the integrationists' claim that, on the basis of their experience, the talking therapies are God's blessing for all mankind. The danger of this flawed theology is that it allows those who claim special knowledge, on the basis of their experience, to declare any therapy they happen to like to be part of common grace. There will undoubtedly be some 'Christian' doctor who will declare that Freud's psychoanalysis, which makes some people feel better, is part of God's common grace. There will be some 'Christian' doctor who will assert that Carl Rogers' non-directive counselling, which helps women feel good about their decision to have an abortion, is part of common grace. It is not difficult to see that this way of thinking is the pathway to licentiousness in the church. The emptiness of the common grace argument is not difficult to see. Those who use it are simply trying to justify their commitment to integrating secular psychotherapy into the church.

God's covenant with his people

When God delivered Israel from the pollution of Egypt's idolatry and superstition, he commanded them to keep themselves separate from the gods of the surrounding nations and to have nothing to do with the detestable practices of idolatry. 'You shall not go after other gods, the gods of the peoples who are all around you' *(Deuteronomy 6.14)*. Yet the Israelites were not satisfied with God's provision in the wilderness and longed for the fleshpots of the Egyptians. So they said to one another, 'Let us select a leader and return to Egypt' *(Numbers 14.4)*. This was a great sin against the God of Heaven, and not one of the Israelites who rebelled against God entered the Promised Land.

The integrationists are those who resort to the fleshpots of Egypt. They are not satisfied with God's provision; they feel they must supplement God's Word with the wisdom of the world. They find it necessary to have communion with the dark teachings of the giants of psychology. But Scripture makes it clear that Christians are not to be yoked together with unbelievers. 'For what fellowship has righteousness with lawlessness? And what communion has light with darkness?' Therefore Christians are to come out from among them and be separate. We are not to touch what is unclean *(2 Corinthians 6.14, 17).*

The church of the living God is the pillar and foundation of truth in this world. Christians are indwelt by the Spirit of Truth. The true church will have nothing to do with the views of those who entirely reject the biblical teaching of morals and personality. It is unthinkable that their teachings can be integrated with God's Word. Those who do so are either being deceived by the false philosophy of this world, or they are false teachers who are deliberately introducing destructive heresy into the church.

God has chosen what appear to be foolish things, in the eyes of the world, to put to shame the 'wisdom' that comes from the spirit of the age. The Christian church does not receive the spirit of the world, but the Spirit of Truth, who is from God. The task of the church is to expose the folly of the giants of psychotherapy, not to accept their foolish teachings.

11
The Case Against Larry Crabb

I N THE FIRST FOUR CHAPTERS we saw that Christian counselling is based on an approach that integrates the best of psychological theory with Scripture. In the next five chapters we outlined the theories and motivation of the leaders of secular psychology. A recurring theme has been the godlessness of the different strands of psychotherapy. In chapter 10, we saw that the giants of psychology are committed to an atheistic view of man and morals, and are wise only according to the spirit of the age. We must now turn to the Christian counselling world to examine the consequences of an approach that amalgamates Scripture and the theories of secular psychology. Our starting point is to look at the teaching of Dr Lawrence Crabb, one of the leading thinkers in the field of Christian counselling.

Dr Crabb has developed a theory of Christian counselling which has been actively promoted in the church throughout the Western world. He has written over 20 books on the subject, such as *Basic Principles of Biblical Counselling* (1975), *Effective Biblical Counselling* (1977), *Understanding People* (1987), *Inside Out* (1988), *Finding God* (1993), *Hope When You're Hurting* (1996), and *The Pressure's Off* (2002), all of which are highly regarded by the Christian counselling movement. His books have been widely read and are used in theological seminaries around the world. Significantly, Crabb has written the foreword to Selwyn Hughes' book on counselling. There is no doubt that his fingerprints are all over the Christian counselling movement in the UK.

However, Crabb is not without his critics. Martin and Deidre Bobgan have severely criticised his work in *Larry Crabb's Gospel* (1998). The Bobgans believe that Crabb's amalgamation of psychology with the Bible impinges on the Gospel message. 'Crabb interprets the message of the cross according to his psychological ideas about the nature of man and how he changes. The Gospel becomes the good news that Jesus meets the needs, longings, passions which motivate all behaviour from the unconscious. Sin becomes wrong strategies for meeting the needs, longings, passions. Confession is telling our stories and gaining insight into those wrong strategies. Full repentance comes through getting in touch with the pain of the past. Hence, the Gospel message itself is directly tied to a psychological construct.'[1] The Bobgans conclude that Crabb's Gospel message itself is directly based on the teaching of psychology rather than Scripture. Because of his position on psychotherapy and its underlying psychologies, Crabb is guilty of *psychoheresy*.[2]

'Effective Biblical Counselling'

In *Effective Biblical Counselling* (1977) Crabb makes it clear that he believes in integrating Scripture and psychotherapy. He explains that counselling involves a stripping away of the layers to reach the real person underneath. 'The context of all such efforts must be genuine acceptance or, as Rogers puts it, unconditional positive regard for the worth of the individual. When the person inside is reached, the truths of Scripture need to be presented in a way suited to the individual's condition . . . The thoroughly qualified biblical counsellor is one who draws upon true knowledge wherever he can find it and one who knows how to approach the unique individual before him to reach him with that truth.'[3] Crabb rejects what he labels the 'Nothing Buttery' (nothing but Scripture) approach that uses only Scripture as simplistic, for it rejects all knowledge from secular sources as tainted and reduces the counselling situation to an identify-confront-change model.

Crabb calls his model of integration 'Spoiling the Egyptians'. 'When

Moses led the children of Israel out of Egyptian bondage, he took freely of the goods of the Egyptians to sustain God's people on their journey to the Promised Land.'[4] While admitting that spoiling the Egyptians is a risky task with real dangers, he argues, 'we can profit from secular psychology if we carefully screen our concepts to determine their compatibility with Christian presuppositions'.[5] As an example, Crabb mentions that 'Albert Ellis, psychologist and proclaimed atheist, has observed that the sentences a person tells himself have a great deal to do with how he thinks and feels. This idea is consistent with Scripture's emphasis on changing your mind in order to act differently (see *Romans 12.1*).'[6] Crabb makes the remarkable claim that Ellis, the founder of Rational Emotive Behavioural Therapy (see chapter 9), who asserts that devout faith in God leads to poor emotional health, has elaborated an important biblical principle.

Crabb's use of Scripture to justify his integration model is highly suspect. It was not God's intention that the Israelites should absorb the culture and religious practices of the Egyptians. On the contrary, the biblical principle is that God's people should be separate and not defile themselves with the idols of Egypt. Israel sinned against God when they 'did not all cast away the abominations which were before their eyes, nor did they forsake the idols of Egypt' *(Ezekiel 20.8)*. Scripture teaches that Christians should not be unequally yoked together with unbelievers. God's people are not to follow the ways and ideas of the world, for friendship with the world of unbelief is enmity against God *(James 4.4)*.

Crabb's psychological model

Crabb outlines his psychological model in *Effective Biblical Coun-selling*. 'People have one basic personal need which requires two kinds of input for its satisfaction. The most basic need is a sense of personal worth, an acceptance of oneself as a whole, real person. The required inputs are significance (purpose, importance, adequacy for a job, meaningfulness, impact) and security (love – unconditional and consistently expressed; permanent acceptance).'[7] According to Crabb, before the Fall Adam and Eve were both significant and secure. The effect of the Fall was to make Adam and Eve feel insecure and insignifi-cant. Crabb's thesis is that problems develop when the basic needs for significance and security are threatened. 'People pursue irresponsible ways of living as a means of defending against feelings of insignificance and insecurity. In most cases these folks have arrived at a wrong idea as to what constitutes significance and security. And these false beliefs are at the core of their problems.'[8] Crabb has based his interpretation of the Fall on Adler's psychological theories. Scripture, however, teaches that the effect of the Fall is that man became separated from God and a slave to sin.

Crabb says that to understand any unit of behaviour, 'we must know what is motivating the behaviour, the person's ideas about what would meet the need, the goal which his thinking has determined as desirable, and the success or failure of the person in reaching the goal.'[9] Crabb explains, 'I am motivated to meet a need by doing certain things which I believe in my mind will meet that need. Motivated behaviour always is directed toward a goal. I believe that something will meet my need. That something becomes my goal . . . when I cannot have what I think I need to be significant or secure, I feel worthless.'[10] This way of thinking is based on Adler's idea that a final goal motivates human behaviour.

As we saw in chapter 7, Crabb lines his theory up with Maslow's hierarchy of needs. He says that Maslow's third and fourth needs (love and purpose) correspond to the personal needs of man: security and significance. Self-actualisation, the ultimate and highest need in Maslow's system, comes close to the biblical concept of becoming mature in Christ.[11]

Crabb argues that for Christians to be well adjusted they must reach the stage of self-actualisation. The first four stages of Maslow's hierarchy of needs must be met, 'then only a Christian has the resources to reach the fifth stage, to actualise himself, and therefore to be truly well-adjusted'. Crabb continues, 'If my reasoning is correct, Christians should be the most self-actualised people around . . . sit down with your Bible and find verses which claim that God has promised to meet every need on Maslow's list.'[12] Crabb reassures the Christian that if the Bible says our psychological needs are met, then they are met. 'Psychotherapy in its most sophisticated form deals with those inaccurate perceptions and helps a person change them to square with Scripture.'[13]

Crabb has introduced Maslow's worldview into the Christian church. He has accepted at face value Maslow's hierarchy of needs and is promoting the concept of self-actualisation among Christians. Yet Maslow's ideas are fundamentally anti-biblical and heavily influenced by New Age thinking. Maslow does his best to explain away the Christian faith – he denies the God of the Bible, and seeks to place autonomous man on the throne. And yet Crabb is eager to promote Maslow's godless ideas among Christians!

Crabb's admiration for Freud

Crabb acknowledges that 'Freud is rightly credited with introducing the whole idea of *psychodynamics* to the modern mind. The term refers to psychological forces within the personality (usually unconscious) that have the power to cause behavioural and emotional disturbance. He taught us to regard problems as *symptoms* of underlying *dynamic processes* in the psyche'[14] (his italics). The aim of psychotherapy is to probe beneath present concerns to expose an unconscious network of defences, anxieties and painful feelings which generate the overt problem. Crabb argues that 'Freud was correct on at least three counts. He was right when he told us that we should look beneath surface problems to hidden internal causes. The Bible describes our hearts as deceitful, so much so that we regularly are not aware of our own motives *(Jeremiah 17.9)* ... Freud also insisted (I think properly) that in order to deal effectively and thoroughly with people, one must have a rather clear understanding of how human nature functions on the inside, where it is not possible to observe directly *(Proverbs 20.5)*. Third, Freud was right in thinking that one necessary means of understanding other people's dynamics is first to understand your own *(Matthew 7.3-5)*. It is for this reason that in most training programmes every student who wants to do psychoanalysis must first be analysed.'[15]

Crabb insists that Freud's error 'is not an insistence that we pay close attention to unconscious forces within personality' but his refusal to study and accept a biblical view of man. The tragedy, according to Crabb, is that there are so few thinkers 'who believe both that an understanding of dynamic functioning is important and that the Bible is an adequate guide for the task.'[16] In other words, there is a need for more Christians who appreciate the value of Freud's teaching on psychotherapy.

In an attempt to gain biblical support for Freud's teaching on the unconscious, Crabb argues that the Greek word *phronema* is translated as 'mind' in *Romans 8*. 'From my study of these passages, it appears that the central concept expressed by the word is a part of personality which develops and holds on to deep, reflective assumptions . . . Let me tentatively suggest that this concept corresponds closely to what psychologists call the "unconscious mind".'[17] On the basis of this interpretation of Scripture, Crabb continues, 'each of us has been programmed in his or her unconscious mind to believe that happiness, worth, joy – all the good things of life – depend upon something other than God.'[18]

But Crabb's interpretation is wide of the mark. The word *phronema* 'denotes what one has in the mind, the thought, or an object of thought'.[19] In *Romans 8.27* the word *phronema* is used of the mind of the Holy Spirit. There is not the slightest hint that the apostle Paul, when he used the word *phronema*, was teaching about the unconscious. On the contrary, Paul is saying that the carnally minded 'set their minds on the things of the flesh' *(Romans 8.5)*. William Hendriksen explains the verse, 'They set their minds on – are most deeply interested in, constantly talk about, engage and glory in – the things pertaining to the flesh, that is, to sinful human nature.'[20] This Scripture does not support the concept of an unconscious mind. So there is no support for Crabb's unorthodox interpretation of Scripture. He has twisted Scripture in an attempt to make Freud's dogma of the unconsciousness appear to have biblical support.

Crabb claims that his understanding 'of unconscious elements within the personality is rooted in the biblical teaching that, above all else, our hearts are deceitful and desperately wicked.'[21] He uses the metaphor of an iceberg, commonly used by secular psychoanalysts, to explain the unconscious. 'Above the waterline are conscious behaviours, beliefs, and emotions. Below the waterline is a network of images and beliefs which we choose to hold but which we refuse to identify clearly. We direct our lives according to a set of ideas of which we remain largely unaware.'[22]

He argues that unless 'we understand sin is rooted in unconscious beliefs and motives and figure out how to expose and deal with these deep forces within the personality the church will continue to promote superficial adjustment while psychotherapists with or without biblical foundations will do a better job than the church of restoring troubled people to more effective functioning. And this is a pitiful tragedy.'[23] The Lord expects more from his people 'than cleaning up their visible acts. He intends us to do more than sweep the streets. He wants us to climb down into the sewers and do something about the filth beneath the concrete. He directs us to enter the dark regions of our soul to find light, to experience his presence when we feel most alone.'[24]

Following Freud's teaching, Crabb offers this advice. 'Think of yourself as an iceberg. Let the visible peak above the waterline represent the things you do, the thoughts you consciously think, and the feelings you sense within you. Let the great mass beneath the waterline represent the part of you that cannot be clearly seen; the motives and attitudes of your heart, those strange impulses that sometimes overwhelm your determination to resist them, the painful memories and raging emotions you prefer to keep hidden beneath the surface of your life.'[25]

The above discussion is extremely important for it tells us much about Crabb's view of Freud, and also of the way he uses Scripture. He is clearly committed to the Freudian view of the unconscious, and is prepared to misuse Scripture in an attempt to rationalise his position. The idea of sin above and below the waterline has no basis in Scripture. Crabb is not 'spoiling' Freud but making him an idol. A feature of Crabb's writing is that he makes frequent references to Scripture in an attempt to justify his theories. But he never starts with Scripture, but always with the psychological theory he seeks to justify. His approach is to search for a Bible verse to support what he is saying. The result is that Scripture is quoted out of context and twisted as he seeks to provide biblical authority for his theories.

As we saw in chapter 3, Crabb is frustrated that many evangelical Christians are sceptical when psychologists go on about the unconscious. The result is that evangelical Christians ignore the sin that lies in the unconscious and only minister above the waterline by studying the Scriptures, exhorting Christians to behave consistently with God's commandments regardless of the emotions that they feel.[26] In Crabb's view, a major error of evangelical churches is a shallow understanding of sin, for many pastors preach an 'iceberg view of sin'.[27] A great mass of sinful beliefs and misdirected motives are never dealt with under this approach. In Crabb's mind this approach is disastrous, for 'pastors and other Christian leaders who work only above the waterline produce either robots or rebels . . . the congregation overflows with Pharisees, people who above the waterline are clean and spiritual but who below the waterline are filled with unrecognised corruption. We must learn to deal with problems below the waterline that typically remain unidentified but still have serious effects on how we live.'[28] Of course, only psychoanalysis can identify the problems that lie below the waterline.

It is not difficult to see that Crabb is an avid disciple of Freud. He teaches that no one can live a victorious Christian life without a therapist delving into the recesses of their unconscious. The Gospel of Christ is only able to deal with sin above the waterline; Freud's psychoanalysis is needed to deal with the sin that lies below the waterline. This is not only profound nonsense, it is false teaching. According to Scripture, 'the word of God is living and powerful, and sharper than any two-edged sword, piercing even to the division of soul and spirit, and of joints and marrow, and is a discerner of the thoughts and intents of the heart' *(Hebrews 4.12)*. It is the Word of God that exposes the thoughts and intents of the human heart. It exposes sin in our inward parts and calls for true repentance. To advocate that Christians need the teaching of Freud to become truly godly is another gospel.

The ineffective church

A theme that runs through Crabb's writings is that the church is ineffective because it has not taken the teachings of Freud to heart. The Christian church is in a state of denial. 'We learn to cooperate in a conspiracy of pretence, to keep our lives polished on the outside, and to deny both the emptiness and bitterness and discontent on the inside as well as our relational ineffectiveness and lack of real intimacy with others.'[29] Churches have become 'polite societies with strict rules of etiquette designed to maintain our denial of who we really are and what problems we are facing. The result is a stiff, cold orthodoxy that squeezes the very life out of Scripture . . . we must face the reality beneath the surface of our lives.'[30] Until the church faces up to the truth that people need to change inside and out, 'we are doing little more than preaching the Gospel and instructing converts in an orthodoxy which requires them to *pretend* [Crabb's italics] that they have been transformed.'[31]

In Crabb's mind the church, obsessed with the superficial message of salvation, does not deal with the real problems that people face. This means that many so-called Christians are living a lie. Most Christians 'cope with life by pretending. We pretend that what we have satisfies more than it does. We pretend we haven't been hurt as badly as we have.'[32] Christians are pretending that they have joy in Christ, whereas the truth is that they are still bound by all the sin and evil that lurks in their as yet untouched unconscious. A Christian cannot be truly liberated when the inner pain and depravity that still resides below the waterline is left undisturbed. The consequence is that conservative Christians are phonies. All their talk about joy in Christ is simply a cliché that has no reality.

Using the teaching of Jesus from *John 7.37* ('if anyone thirsts, let him come to Me'), Crabb has built an elaborate dogma that asserts that all people have deep unsatisfied thirsts or longings. This idea is similar to Maslow's hierarchy of needs which portrays man as a wanting, needy animal. Crabb writes, 'Only God can supply what my soul most deeply desires, when crucial longings are not satisfied, there is pain that must be dealt with . . . Without Someone who cares and something to do that matters, life is an unspeakably cruel experience to be avoided, distorted or denied.'[33] Christians who do not admit the painfulness of unsatisfied thirst violate love in order to protect themselves from personal pain, and fall into the subtle sin of self-protection. Therefore in order to 'deeply understand sin – the ways in which we violate love – we must first become aware of our thirst'.[34] Christians who stay away from their hurt tend to develop a matter-of-fact relationship with Christ, while those who 'embrace their hurt are able to pursue God more passionately'.[35]

So what must we do? The advice from Crabb is that we must 'ask tough questions that produce confusion . . . sincere questions spoken from a heart of pain must be allowed to open the door to confusion. To slam the door shut, and in so doing to assert that honest confusion has no place in our pursuit of God, leads to a forced, mechanical trust rather than to a real and vital confidence.'[36] Crabb claims that an honest look at life will produce confusion. 'But confusion isn't bad, it's good, because in the middle of confusion we become aware of a passionate desire to know that Someone strong and kind is working behind all we see, moving things carefully toward a just and joyful conclusion.'[37] Crabb asserts that faith develops 'when our mind is so troubled by confusion that we either believe God or give up on life. Letting our self experience confusion creates a thirst that only faith can satisfy.'[38]

Who is the god who wants confusion among his followers? Certainly not the God of the Bible, for he is a God of order. Confusion is a feature of pagan worship. 'For God is not the author of confusion but of peace, as in all the churches of the saints' *(1 Corinthians 14.33)*. Advising the people of God to open the door to confusion is to invite evil influences into the church.

The new birth is not enough

According to Crabb, Christians lack a coherent model of change. Crabb asks how a hot-tempered parent develops patience with his irritating children. How does a woman who feels sexually aroused by another woman convert to heterosexuality? 'But beyond a few basic ideas about obedience, prayer and time in the Word, we're not very clear about how change occurs or what prompts it.'[39] And if we were to ask church leaders we are not likely to receive a satisfactory reply either. 'It is very likely that you will hear a lot of tired clichés about the power of God and his Word that upon inspection are found to say very little. We really don't have a clear idea about the solutions to people's problems that we can translate into specific strategies for helping people.'[40] Because he believes the Bible is ineffective in changing people, Crabb argues that the church needs a counselling model to facilitate the profound change that Christians really need. 'There are technical understandings of psychological dynamics and therapeutic procedures which add greatly to counselling effectiveness.'[41] Effective Christian counselling, Crabb says, will lead to 'a tremendous increase in spiritual and emotional maturity in our churches'.[42]

In his book *Finding God* (1993), Crabb is dismissive of those who insist that the new birth gets rid of all the vicious arrogance that defines the old nature.[43] Crabb believes that our fallen nature survives the new birth, so we need something more. We need a revolution to dismantle the fallen structure and replace it with a godly structure. Crabb claims that fallen structures remain undisturbed in many born-again Christians. The narrow gate toward God, which many Christians have never walked through, opens when we believe that God is good no matter what happens in our life. 'When he [the Holy Spirit] ushers us into the presence of ultimate goodness, when our darkest tragedy is pierced by one glimpse of invisible glory, then faith is born.'[44]

Crabb believes when young people decide to follow Christ good things happen. There may well be outward signs of their inward faith, as their lifestyle is changed. The flight from lust, the avoidance of the appearance of evil, and separation from the things of the world 'are more the fruit of coming to Christ than the core . . . But much more is involved in changing from the inside out than pulling rotten fruit off the tree.'[45] When the battle is fought by trying to do what the Bible commands, eventual defeat is guaranteed, because we have not dealt with sin in the heart.

Crabb explains that there are two kinds of sin. The first is visible acts of transgression against biblical standards. This is the sin that evangelical Christians focus on. The second kind of sin is a subtle violation of our Lord's command to love, and this is the real sin in the heart.[46] The greatest sin, in Crabb's eyes, is the sin of self-protection. Christians are self-protective in the way they relate to other people. When we try to protect ourselves from personal pain, by denying our deepest unsatisfied longings, we commit the subtle sin of self-protection. When we act in a way to avoid our inner pain, we wrap ourselves in the sin of self-protection which stains our best efforts to love.[47] According to Crabb, 'We will not recognise the subtle sin of self-protection until we realise the pain from which we want to protect our self.'[48] While the church concentrates on sins of behaviour, like adultery, stealing and lying, it fails to address the greatest sin of all, self-protection, which Crabb tries to define with his counselling stories. The sin of self-protection can only be exorcised by psychotherapy. To change from the inside out we must repent of our self-protection commitment.[49]

The problem with Crabb's subtle sin of self-protection, which has its roots below the waterline, is that it is so subtle that Christians are not aware of the sin until they undergo psychoanalysis. By this logic, only those Christians who have been counselled can overcome this evil. It is significant that Crabb describes the sin of self-protection as the great sin, while he seems to think that obeying God's law is of secondary importance.

According to Crabb, salvation from sin depends on more than Christ. He does not appear to accept that if a person is in Christ, he is a new creation, old things have passed away, and all things have become new (2 Corinthians 5.17). In Crabb's eyes true salvation is only achieved by those who have found Christ and have had the sin of self-protection dealt with by psychotherapy.

Crabb's pathway to God

In *Finding God*, Crabb (after two decades as a teacher of Christian counselling) revealed the entry in his journal which described his struggle to find God. According to Crabb the road to finding God takes us through darkness before it brings us to light. 'Sometimes my soul feels dead. Other times tortured. Right now I feel a terrible combination of both . . . is there enough left of me to continue on . . . or have I disappeared into a cave of dark, tangled tunnels, a cold black maze that angles downward from which I will never emerge . . . Where's God? What's he supposed to be doing? I want to move, to choose something aggressively. But a deep, angry boredom, a hopeless indifference, has robbed me of energy.'[50] Crabb writes that to move at all, he must believe two things: one, that he exists beneath his pain as a free person who can move, and two, that there really is an infinitely good Person who invites him to move toward a joy that he provides.[51] Crabb goes on, 'I believe God exists. And I believe I exist. I can't get away from the idea of a personal energy outside of myself big enough to hem me in. I can think of this personal reality as good or bad, but I can't envision his (not its) absence, his nonexistence. Someone is there! Final reality is personal.'[52]

Crabb then poses this question. Is this Final Person good or bad? And he envisions 'that Person moving towards me and feeling something for me as he comes closer.'[53] He then has a strangely unshakeable conviction that this Ultimate Person is the God of the Bible, the God revealed in Jesus Christ. 'If I make myself ask why I believe God is good, why the Supreme Being is not bad, my attention goes quickly to my thirst for beauty: the beauty of love, the beauty of order, the beauty of joy. I know the lust for beauty is within me – I can't get away from it. And I know it is a good lust, one that I can never eliminate.'[54] Remarkable that Crabb, who claims to be a Christian, turns to himself (his thirst for beauty), not to the Cross of Christ, to understand that God is good.

Crabb then faces the question, what will this God do with him, someone who refuses to trust his goodness? 'The moment I ask that question with the urgency it deserves, something happens. It is then that

I catch a glimpse of God's blazing glory. What has he done with me? He accepts me! He loves me! That glimpse gives me a taste of him, and I know that he is good beyond every imagination . . . As I ponder the relationship between God and me – one that he has arranged – I sense the stirrings of hope. I see light. The cave is still black, but I am no longer falling more deeply into it. Through no power of mine, I feel myself being lifted out of it. I find myself walking in a meadow blooming with wild flowers, moving towards a stream of clear water, then lying down beside it on a grassy bank. The sun is shining, warming my body, while a gentle breeze keeps me from becoming uncomfortably hot. And I am aware of the sheer joy of being alive. I seem to be resting and moving at the same time, resting in Christ and moving toward him, farther and farther away from the black hole that so recently has been my prison.'[55]

Then something happens, some disturbing news, and 'in an instant the grassy bank disappears and I am again plummeting into darkness. Again my soul feels dead, tortured, alive only with pain and doubt.'[56]

This is Crabb's description of his pathway to God. But here we must ask, 'Who is the Final Person that revealed himself to Crabb?' Is the God that Crabb met in his mystical experience truly the God of the Bible? It sounds more like a New Age experience of enlightenment, or a peak-experience as described by Maslow. It is a fair question to ask whether Crabb truly understands the Christian Gospel. How much faith can we have in a man who has such an uncertain knowledge of Christian conversion?

In his book *The Pressure's Off* (2002) Crabb tries to persuade us not to follow what he labels the Old Way of obedience to biblical principles, but the New Way of experiencing God. In the book Crabb describes another ecstatic experience. This time the Spirit of God speaks to him: 'I want to tell you something. I want to tell you what you've been wanting to know.' Crabb describes how he heard a Voice from Heaven reaching into his cave. 'Larry, there's a new way to live . . . It's time! It's time to leave the Old Way that's causing you so much pressure – having to keep people happy with you, having to succeed in your relationships and ministry, having to feel at least a little good – and to live the New Way, the way my blood has opened to you. Larry, come out of the cave. It's time!' Here we have the leader of the Christian counselling movement telling us that a Voice from Heaven had to point him to the New Way.

Scripture, it appears, is not sufficient to teach him how he ought to follow Christ. He needs a special revelation! The fact that Crabb claims that God speaks to him suggests that he is a modern-day prophet. Are we really to believe that a man who follows the teachings of Freud and Maslow is a prophet from God? Are we really to believe that the God of the Bible delivers personal messages to Larry Crabb?

Melvin Tinker's incisive review of *The Pressure's Off* concludes that by a combination of woolly thinking, sloppy argument and bad exegesis, Crabb is substituting mysticism for biblical Christianity. 'Ironically, the "new way" of Crabb is nothing less than the "old way" of works-orientated mystical Catholicism with its use of spiritual directors, techniques and the like . . . The very thing Paul condemns in *Galatians* (which Crabb refers to but misunderstands), the loss of liberty in Christ, is the destination to which Crabb is heading and leading others.

'Crabb badly handles Scripture throughout this volume. For example, he quotes *1 John* about the "anointing of the Spirit", which Crabb argues is something we should seek, while John is reminding Christians that this is what they already have. Such a loose handling of Scripture is surely lamentable . . . This is a book not to be commended except as a warning of what happens when subjective experience replaces the objective teaching of the Bible.'[57]

The legacy of Larry Crabb

In the previous chapter we saw that the giants of psychotherapy (Freud, Adler, Maslow, Rogers and Ellis) are scoffers who have set themselves against the God of the Bible – they are the enemies of the Gospel of Christ. Scripture instructs God's people to have 'no fellowship with the unfruitful works of darkness, but rather expose them' *(Ephesians 5.11)*. Yet Larry Crabb is not only comfortable working with the psychological theories that come from the darkened minds of the giants of anti-Christian psychology, but is integrating their foolish teaching into the church.

Crabb's model of Christian counselling is essentially Freudian in concept, although he has attempted to disguise this connection beneath a veneer of Christian terminology. Crabb teaches that human behaviour is controlled by unconscious dynamic forces that even the new birth in Christ is not enough to overcome – we need psychotherapy to uncover the sins of which we are unaware. In the face of God's promise, that if we confess our sins, he will forgive our sins and cleanse us from *all* unrighteousness *(1 John 1.9)*, Crabb asserts that only psychoanalysis can deal with the sin that lies below the waterline in our unconscious mind.

Crabb's theology of need places man at the centre. God's chief purpose is to meet the needs and longings of thirsty men and women, and to provide them with a sense of security and significance. The role of the counsellor is to help Christians understand the unmet needs that are causing their inner hurt. Crabb has placed enormous power in the hands of the counselling movement, for only it has the esoteric knowledge to deal with the difficult spiritual and emotional problems that Christians face.

It is not difficult to see that Crabb's teaching presents a false view of the nature and character of God. He uses New Age terms – 'a personal energy', 'a Final Person', 'the Ultimate Person', 'Someone beyond ourselves', 'the Supreme Being', 'the Voice' to refer to God. Crabb claims to know that God is good because of his (Crabb's) lust for beauty, not because God has revealed his holy, righteous character in Scripture and through the incarnate Christ.

Crabb's model of Christian counselling diminishes the moral law of God, and downplays the importance of obedience to God's commandments. It rejects the sufficiency of Christ in all things pertaining to life and holiness. It does not accept that suffering for the Gospel is part of the Christian life. It twists Scripture to support the theories of secular psychotherapy.

There is no doubt that Larry Crabb's thinking has had a large influence on the Christian counselling movement. He has been massively influential in inculcating the ideas of secular psychology into the church. And so we must ask, is this man a prophet or a charlatan? A deep Christian thinker or a New Age mystic? Is he a man of God, with a profound commitment to building the church of Christ, or a false teacher who is using the Christian faith for his own purposes?

12
Self-esteem: the Secular Foundation

THE SELF-ESTEEM MOVEMENT has gained enormous influence over the last three decades in both the secular and Christian worlds. It is widely accepted that low self-esteem is the cause of all kinds of social and behavioural problems, from unwanted teenage pregnancies, to poor school performance, to drug abuse. The dogma of self-esteem lies at the heart of the Christian counselling movement. There are literally hundreds of Christian self-help books that point to the importance of healthy self-esteem as a necessary ingredient for a successful life. Parents are taught techniques for enhancing their children's self-esteem.

Psychologist Dr Nathaniel Branden has been at the forefront of the self-esteem movement. In *Psychology of Self-Esteem*, originally published in 1969, he explains how self-esteem – or lack of it – affects our values, responses, and goals. He is the author of many books on self-esteem including the perennially best-selling *How to Raise your Self-Esteem* (1987), *The Six Pillars of Self-Esteem* (1995) and *A Woman's Self-Esteem* (1998).

Branden defines self-esteem as the 'experience of being competent to cope with the basic challenges of life and of being worthy of happiness'.

He sees self-esteem as a basic human need that is essential to normal and healthy development. Lacking positive self-esteem leads to stunted psychological growth. 'If we do not believe in ourselves – neither in our efficacy nor in our goodness (and lovability) – the world is a frightening place . . . The first love affair we must consummate successfully in this world is with ourselves; only then are we ready for a relationship.' To be self-responsible we must recognise that we are the authors of our choices and actions, 'that we must be the ultimate source of our own fulfillment; that no one is coming to make our life right for us, or make us happy, or give us self-esteem.'[1]

In the three decades since *The Psychology of Self-Esteem* was first published psychologists, counsellors, educators, and the general public worldwide have come to appreciate the supposed value of healthy self-esteem. The self-esteem movement has fundamentally transformed our culture. In America the propagation of healthy self-esteem has taken on all the fervour of a religious movement. People are being led to believe that self-esteem has profound consequences for every aspect of their existence. For the individual it is seen as the way to a happy, meaningful and productive life; for society it is the answer to most social problems. How we function in the workplace, how we deal with other people, how we make a success of life are all dependent on being in possession of healthy self-esteem. It is widely believed that our level of self-esteem even influences our choice of partner, how we relate with our partner, children, and friends, and, ultimately, what level of personal happiness we attain in this life.

Such is the American obsession with self-esteem that in 1987 the State of California set up the Task Force for Self-Esteem and Personal and Social Responsibility. Its final report *Toward a State of Self-Esteem* (1990) concluded, 'Self-esteem is the likeliest candidate for a social vaccine, something that empowers us to live responsibly and that inoculates us against the lures of crime, violence, substance abuse, teen pregnancy, child abuse, chronic welfare dependency, and educational failure. The lack of self-esteem is central to most personal and social ills plaguing our state and nation.'[2] So profound is belief in self-esteem dogma that it is seen as the answer to most social problems, for those with healthy self-esteem will be able to overcome the temptation to indulge in crime, drugs, promiscuous sex and much more.

In 1995 the National Association for Self-Esteem in the USA (NASE) declared that its mission was 'to promote awareness of and provide vision, leadership and advocacy for improving the human condition through the enhancement of healthy self-esteem'. The National Association invites us to 'join hands now with individuals from around the country and around the world who are committed to integrating self-esteem into the fabric of our society'.[3]

NASE is dedicated to improving the quality of life by integrating self-esteem into the fabric of American society, so that the development of personal worth, responsibility, and integrity become paramount and commonplace in families, schools, the workplace, and the government. The President of NASE issued a challenge to its members. 'Do something each day that promotes your healthy self-esteem and helps others develop self-confidence, pride and self-respect.'[4]

In the UK the self-esteem movement, which has made large advances in the last three decades, received great encouragement with the establishment of the Government's Social Exclusion Unit in 1997. The Unit, set up to tackle social deprivation, readily accepted policy initiatives from the USA that depicted low self-esteem as both the cause and effect of social exclusion and educational disadvantage. Reports by the Social Exclusion Unit have influenced many areas of education policy. The Government has eagerly ploughed significant amounts of funding into initiatives to improve self-esteem among school children. The Conservative party leader, David Cameron, in calling for governments to foster emotional well-being, is the latest to join the bandwagon.

Yet the claim that low self-esteem is the cause of social and behavioural problems is not backed up by sound research. According to Kathryn Ecclestone, professor of education at Oxford Brookes University, 'A lack of robust research does not stop the Department for Education and Skills making sweeping assertions about links between poor emotional literacy, crime, marriage breakdown, offending, antisocial behaviour, disruption in schools and mental health. These are translated into official targets and guidance for "social, emotional and affective learning" in primary schools, soon to be extended into secondary schools.'[5] A deluge of guidance is directed at teaching school children the skills of emotional literacy. An important school initiative is circle time – in many primary schools this has become a therapeutic ritual that encourages children to talk about their feelings, and helps them to feel good about themselves.

Despite the lack of evidence to support the claims of the self-esteem lobby, it is widely accepted by politicians and opinion formers that low self-esteem is associated with all manner of behavioural problems and social ills. The Teenage Parenthood Working Group, for example, claims that the reason young people make unhealthy sexual choices is because they have low self-esteem. 'Young people with positive self-esteem are much less likely to become teenage parents. Efforts to reduce teenage parenthood rates in both the short and long term must focus on improving self-esteem among young people.'[6] Sex education encourages the idea that positive self-esteem helps young people make healthy sexual choices. There is now a self-esteem industry which uses a whole range of techniques for helping people develop positive self-esteem, including psychotherapy, cognitive therapy, hypnosis, Reike and various other New Age techniques.

The roots of self-esteem dogma

The self-esteem movement has its roots in the teachings of the humanist psychologists. In *A Theory of Human Motivation* Maslow emphasised the need for self-esteem. He claimed that all people have a need for a stable, firmly based, high evaluation of themselves. 'Satisfaction of the self-esteem need leads to feelings of self-confidence, worth, strength, capability and adequacy of being useful and necessary in the world. But thwarting of these needs produces feelings of inferiority, of weakness and of helplessness. These feelings in turn give rise to either basic discouragement or else compensatory or neurotic trends.'[7]

Maslow described a positive, self-actualising force within each person that is struggling to assert itself. He believed that since our 'inner nature is good or neutral rather than bad, it is best to bring it out and encourage it rather than to suppress it. If it is permitted to guide our life, we grow healthy, fruitful, and happy.'[8] In *Unmasking the New Age* Douglas Groothuis points out that Maslow, an atheist, has invested humanity with the attributes of deity. 'Maslow's path breaking efforts cleared the way for an exodus from the old psychological view of humanity toward a new human that is essentially good and has within himself unlimited potential for growth. A whole host of thinkers – Erich Fromm, Rollo

May, Carl Rogers and others – sound this call. In humanistic psychology the self is seen as the radiant heart of health, and psychotherapy must strive to get the person in touch with that source of goodness . . . This is the message at the core of New Age teaching.'[9]

The ideas of Carl Rogers have had a large impact on the self-esteem movement. He believed that human nature is basically good. Every human, therefore, should feel good about himself, and accept himself as he is. The need for 'positive self-regard' is essential for a person to be psychologically healthy. According to Rogers, human beings value positive self-regard, self-esteem, self-worth and a positive self-image. Lack of self-esteem hinders our psychological growth and prevents us from developing our full potential.

A massive self-esteem industry that has invaded virtually every aspect of life, including the arenas of education, health, religion and commerce, has been erected on the theoretical foundation of humanistic psychology. The trumpet call of the self-esteem movement has been sounded, warning of the scourge of low self-esteem that threatens all people. Gloria Steinem's bestseller, *Revolution from Within*, is a book about self-esteem. In her preface she writes, 'The more I talked to men as well as women, the more it seemed that inner feelings of incompleteness, emptiness, self-doubt and self-hatred were the same, no matter who experienced them, and even if they were expressed in culturally opposite ways.' We are told that to function properly we need positive, healthy self-esteem.

'Overcoming Low Self-Esteem'

A popular self-help guide, *Overcoming Low Self-Esteem*, written by Dr Melanie Fennell, a clinical psychologist, 'helps readers to understand their condition, and, armed with new knowledge, to break out of the vicious circle of negative self-image, learn the art of self-acceptance and alter their lives for the better'. It is, in fact, teaching a dogma that aims to change us into better people. The author explains that at the heart of low self-esteem lie negative beliefs about the self, and the judgements we make of ourselves and the worth we place on ourselves as people.[10] Dr Fennell aims 'to undermine the old negative view of yourself and establish and strengthen a more positive, kindly, accepting alternative'.[11]

Experiences during our childhood that have contributed to low self-esteem are failing to meet parental standards, failing to meet peer group standards and the absence of praise and affection, among others.[12] The beliefs we hold about ourselves directly reflect the messages we received as children. We have formed judgements about ourselves as people.[13] These judgements lie at the heart of low self-esteem. Judgements include ideas such as, 'I'm bad, worthless and unacceptable'. The result is that we go through life focusing on what we do wrong, not on what we do right. Our basic beliefs about ourselves are negative.

The author draws attention to the association between low self-esteem and negative beliefs about oneself. In low self-esteem, negative beliefs about the self lead on to self-critical thinking. This contributes to keeping low self-esteem going, because it triggers feelings like guilt, shame and depression. 'People with low self-esteem criticise themselves for all the things they should be doing and aren't – and for all the things they should not be doing and are. People with low self-esteem notice some difficulty or something wrong about themselves, and on that basis make judgements about themselves as whole people ... Self-critical thoughts result in painful feelings (sadness, disappointment, anger, guilt), and keep low self-esteem going.'[14] It is interesting that Dr Fennell's description of low self-esteem is remarkably similar to the experience of the apostle Paul in his struggle against his sinful nature, 'For what I will to do, that I do not practise; but what I hate, that I do ... O wretched man that I am! Who will deliver me from this body of death? I thank God – through Jesus Christ our Lord!' *(Romans 7.15, 24, 25.)*

Rules for living lie at the heart of the problem of low self-esteem. Parents pass on rules to their children and children absorb rules from their families and parents purely by observation.[15] Extreme and unbending rules, that place demands that are impossible to meet, and make no concession to circumstances, create problems.[16] Rules can restrict our freedom to be our true self. We need to formulate new rules which will allow us more freedom of movement and encourage us to accept ourselves just as we are.[17]

Absolute rules are those that do not allow for shades of grey. Absolute rules are reflected in their language: 'I must, I should, I ought to.' Flexible rules, on the other hand, are characterised by: 'It would be in my interests to, or I prefer, I need, I would like to.'[18] The author explains, 'This black-and-white quality may reflect that fact that they [the absolute rules] were developed when you were very young, before you had the breadth of experience to see things from a more complex perspective.'[19]

To enhance self-esteem we are encouraged to overcome our taboo against positive thinking and to recognise that self-acceptance is part of healthy self-esteem. Ignoring the positive contributes to keeping low self-esteem. Making a list of our good qualities is the first step toward enhancing low self-esteem.[20] We need to change our rules for living. 'You are looking for general rules that reflect what you expect of yourself, your standards for who you should be and how you should behave, your sense of what is acceptable and what is not allowed, and your idea of what is necessary in order to succeed in life and achieve satisfying relationships. In essence, you are defining what you have to do or be in order to feel good about yourself, and what your self-esteem depends on.'[21]

Dr Melanie Fennell leaves us in no doubt that absolute rules or laws, such as those in the Bible, are a major cause of our low self-esteem. This is why to enhance our self-esteem we need to develop a flexible set of rules with which we feel comfortable, and which do not judge us too harshly.

Texas University Counselling and Mental Health Centre

Texas University Counselling and Mental Health Centre has a user-friendly brochure that explains self-esteem in a straightforward manner. We are told that 'healthy self-esteem is based on our ability to assess ourselves accurately (know ourselves) and still be able to accept and to value ourselves unconditionally. This means being able to realistically acknowledge our strengths and limitations (which is part of being human) and at the same time accepting ourselves as worthy and worthwhile without conditions or reservations.'

In response to a question about our 'inner voice' the brochure explains that 'our past experiences, even the things we don't usually think about, are all alive and active in our daily life in the form of an inner voice ... For people with healthy self-esteem the messages of the inner voice are positive and reassuring. For people with low self-esteem, the inner voice becomes a harsh inner critic, constantly criticising, punishing, and belittling their accomplishments.' Another term for the inner voice is conscience – it is clear that self-esteem dogma sees our conscience, which warns us when we are doing wrong, as a major problem.

Before we can begin to improve our self-esteem we must first believe that we can change it. 'The first important step in improving self-esteem is to begin to challenge the negative messages of the critical inner voice.' The second step is to begin to treat ourselves as a worthwhile person. 'Start to challenge past negative experiences or messages by nurturing and caring for yourself in ways that show that you are valuable, competent, deserving and lovable.' There are several components to self-nurturing that include: practising basic self-care, planning fun and relaxing things for ourselves, rewarding ourselves for our accomplishments, reminding ourselves of our strengths and achievements, forgiving ourselves when we don't do all we hoped we would do.

Step three is to get help from others. According to the brochure, getting help from others is often the most important step we can take to improve our self-esteem, but it can also be the most difficult. 'Sometimes low self-esteem can feel so painful or difficult to overcome that the professional help of a therapist or counsellor is needed. Talking to a counsellor is a good way to learn more about your self-esteem issues and begin to improve your self-esteem.'

The Kairos Foundation

The Kairos Foundation is an organisation that majors on teaching self-esteem. It was first conceived in 1979 by its co-founders Roy Whitten and Brad Brown as a way to offer the skills and practices they had developed through their own work in psychotherapy and pastoral counselling. The Kairos Foundation aims to empower people everywhere with practices that develop personal potential and help overcome human separateness. Over the past 20 years it has helped many thousands of individuals transform their vision of life, and has worked with schools, universities, graduate programmes, non-governmental organisations and government agencies on four continents.

The Kairos Foundation teaches that the starting point is to recognise that your past, largely through what you were taught by your parents as a child, has shaped your self-esteem. You have developed patterns of behaviour that produce low self-esteem. You may have been cautioned to be humble, to consider your mistakes as bad or wrong, and perhaps your parents' attitude was often one of disapproval. They may have taught you to fear God, and made it hard for you to honour and respect yourself as a person. They had expectations and made demands that you could not meet. You did not really feel loved, wanted or accepted. Your young mind formed a judgement that you are not worthwhile as a person and this shaped your self-esteem.

Your mind acts like a bio-computer which controls your behaviour. An inner voice, or mind-talk, has programmed you to behave in a certain way, and this has incapacitated your self-esteem. Your mind threatens you with things you must do, with obligations and inner demands, like inner rules. Your mind-talk is telling you what to do, what to believe, and it is passing judgements on how worthwhile you are as a person. Your inner voice passes judgements that make you feel guilty and bad. This affects your view of yourself as a person, and affects your self-esteem.

The moment you decide to enhance your self-esteem you give your mind the power to be more happy and content than you could ever have imagined. You will realise that you've been a hard taskmaster – that your judgements have been too harsh. The way to enhance your self-esteem is to free yourself from your mind-talk and its inner demands.

A summary of the message of self-esteem

Self-esteem dogma is, root and branch, the construct of humanistic psychology – it has emerged from the minds of Maslow, Fromm and Rogers. The humanists, who believe in the inherent goodness of human nature and reject the concept of sin, need a plausible explanation for the problem of human misery and unhappiness. What they have done is to develop the psychological construct of 'low self-esteem' in an attempt to explain away the effects of sin on the human condition. The essential message of self-esteem dogma can be summarised:

1. Most people feel that there is more to life than is being experienced. This discontentment is characterised by feelings of shame, misery, guilt, sadness and dissatisfaction with relationships. Secular psychologists have coined the term 'low self-esteem' to describe this concept. Scripture teaches that the cause of this discontentment is sin

that separates man from God – there is no rest for the wicked.

2. Feelings of low self-esteem are aggravated by something that is within all people – an inner voice, or our parents' voice or what Kairos refers to as mind-talk. Our inner voice provides a set of standards by which we ought to live and acts as an inner judge that makes us pass judgements on ourselves. Consequently, we are always falling short of our black and white, inflexible standards. This makes us feel that we are a failure, even that we are bad, and sometimes even that we are sinful. Scripture teaches that God has written his law in the human heart, and we have a God-given conscience that reminds us of God's law.

3. Low self-esteem that results from our self-judgement is the cause of many social and behavioural problems. Scripture teaches that sin is the cause of social and behavioural problems.

4. For us to feel better we must enhance our self-esteem. We must reject negative thoughts about ourselves and cultivate more positive thoughts. But this is difficult because our inner voice keeps reminding us of our strict inflexible rules that make us feel guilty. The only way to achieve healthy self-esteem is to reject all ideas about absolute rules and develop flexible rules that do not judge us so harshly, so that we feel good about ourselves. Scripture teaches that the answer to low self-esteem is to receive a new heart by repenting of sin and turning to Christ in faith.

The great fallacy of the self-esteem movement is that it does not acknowledge the effect that sin has on human beings. It also ignores the fact that we all have a God-given conscience that is guided by the moral law that God has put into the hearts of all people *(Romans 2.12-16)*. It is our conscience that warns us when we do wrong, and makes us feel guilty and ashamed. The purpose of self-esteem dogma is to persuade us that we should not listen to our inner voice, that we should ignore the judgement of our conscience. So self-esteem dogma seeks to persuade us that there is no absolute moral law to which we are accountable.

It is not difficult to see the antinomianism that lies behind the self-esteem movement. The daunting challenge is to help sinful people, who are without God and without hope, feel good about themselves. Now that we understand the foundation and purpose of self-esteem dogma, we can turn to the self-esteem message of the Christian counselling movement.

13
Self-esteem and the Christian Counselling Movement

THE DOGMA OF SELF-ESTEEM has been enthusiastically embraced by the Christian counselling movement. There are numerous Christian self-help books that point to the importance of healthy self-esteem as a necessary ingredient for a successful life. A Christian website (Wesley Owen) in the UK lists 36 Christian books that deal with self-esteem – titles include *The Self-Esteem Journal*, *Building Self-Esteem*, *Look Great Feel Great*, *All About Self-Esteem* and so on.

The popular American psychologist Dr James Dobson has probably done more than any other person to introduce the dogma of self-esteem into the church. It is a central theme that runs through most of his books, radio programmes, films, videos and tapes. His ministry, through Focus on the Family, is to provide folksy, psychological advice on how Christians should enhance their self-esteem. He specialises in providing advice for parents on how they should bring up their children. In his book *Hide or Seek*, first published in 1974, Dobson declares that his purpose is 'to formulate a well-defined philosophy – an approach to child rearing – that will contribute to self-esteem from infancy onwards'.[1]

Dobson is surrounded by a great cloud of Christian witnesses who propagate the dogma of self-esteem. Prominent on the self-esteem bandwagon is Robert Schuller the popular TV evangelist. In his book *Self-Esteem: the New Reformation* (1982), Schuller claims that at the core of man's sin is not his depravity but a lack of self-dignity. Self-esteem is feeling good about one's self because one has been working hard and well. He asserts that the opposite of good self-esteem is that which causes a person to say 'I am unworthy', which in Schuller's eyes is the worst sin that a man or woman can commit.[2] He goes so far as to say, 'Sin is any act or thought that robs myself or another human being of his or her self-esteem.'[3] He argues that self-esteem is the single greatest need facing the human race today.

Joel Osteen, pastor of non-denominational Lakewood Church in Houston, is a rising 'star' in the Christian world. His book, *Your Best Life Now: Seven Steps to Living at Your Full Potential* (2004) is a self-help guide to human-potential and self-esteem, which ranks number one on the prestigious *New York Times* best-seller list. Rick Warren of Saddleback Church and author of *The Purpose Driven Life* and Joyce Meyer of the Word and Life Movement both promote self-esteem dogma. Joyce Meyer explains, 'For years I had low self-esteem and I did not like myself.'[4] In her book *Look Great, Feel Great* (2006) 'Joyce addresses the self-esteem drought that leads us to bad health habits'.[5]

Max Lucado, minister of the Oak Hills Church of Christ in San Antonio and a popular author, is a keen advocate of self-esteem dogma. In *Travelling Light* (2001) he poses the question, 'Do you feel a need for affirmation? Does your self-esteem need attention? You don't need to drop names or show off. You need only pause at the base of the cross and be reminded of this: The Maker of the stars would rather die for you than live without you. And that is a fact. So if you need to brag, brag about that.'[6] In the UK, Steve Chalke advises parents on how to help their children develop a positive self-image. Oasis Esteem, a charity founded by Chalke, holds sex education sessions which 'promote young people's self-esteem, assertiveness, negotiation skills and respect for others'.[7] Selwyn Hughes and the CWR are committed to the promotion of self-esteem among Christians.

Critics of self-esteem dogma

Jay E. Adams challenged the foundations of the self-esteem movement in *The Biblical View of Self-Esteem, Self-Love, Self-Worth* (1986).
He writes, 'During the last 15 years we have seen the rise of a powerful
and influential movement within the church. You can easily identify
it by observing the use of one or more of the several closely related
labels with which it is intimately associated: self-image, self-esteem,
self-worth, and self-love. The one common denominator, regardless
of the nomenclature used by any particular advocate of this movement, is the emphasis on self. Such persons regularly speak and write
about "coming to a high view of self," "feeling good about yourself,"
"gaining a sense of personal value and worth," and the like. Whatever
their differences, the one enemy which they are unitedly fighting is *low
self-esteem*.'

Paul Vitz is highly critical of self-esteem dogma which he places very
firmly in the humanist camp. 'Historically selfism derives from an
explicitly anti-Christian humanism and its hostility to Christianity is
a logical expression of its very different assumptions about the nature
of the self, of creativity, of the family, of love and of suffering. In short,
humanistic selfism is not a science but a popular secular substitute
religion, which has nourished and spread today's widespread cult of
self-worship.'[8]

Three sources have been selected to describe what the Christian
counselling movement teaches about self-esteem. The first is a book on
self-esteem published by CWR, the second is David Seamands' best-
seller *Healing Damaged Emotions* and the third is an examination of
James Dobson's teaching.

'Insight into Self-esteem'

The book *Insight into Self-esteem* (2006) is based on one-day seminars held by CWR and is a good example of the Christian counselling
movement's approach to self-esteem.

(i) Christians and low self-esteem

The book starts by explaining that 'it is well acknowledged amongst
psychiatrists and psychologists that healthy self-esteem is critical for

our mental health'.[9] We are told that our self-esteem ebbs and flows as we find ourselves in different situations. 'It contributes to our understanding of the way we view ourselves; the thoughts we have about ourselves and the value we place on ourselves as people . . . Healthy self-esteem is demonstrated when we can say "I'm good, I'm worthwhile." . . . Yet, healthy self-esteem is by no means a natural given. It is, to a large extent, a learnt behaviour.'[10] The challenge is to develop positive self-esteem so that we can live a successful Christian life. According to the authors, the ultimate source of healthy self-esteem is the One who made us. 'God's will for us is that we live in possession of healthy self-esteem . . . By seeking him first, discovering who we really are in God, and letting him meet our needs, our self-esteem can be maintained at a healthy level.'[11]

But Scripture does not teach that it is God's will that we live in possession of healthy self-esteem. Scripture teaches that it is God's will that we should be holy *(1 Thessalonians 4.7)*, that we should walk as Jesus walked *(1 John 2.6)*, that we should obey God's Word, not that we should live in possession of healthy self-esteem. The apostle Paul explained that he counted all things loss for the excellence of the knowledge of Christ Jesus, for whom he had suffered the loss of all things. God does not save us in order that we might have healthy self-esteem, but that we might be transformed into the image of his Son.

(ii) God is mighty to save from a lifetime of low self-esteem

According to the authors, if our standards are 'so high as to be almost unobtainable we will put ourselves forward for failure'.[12] Therefore we need to recognise where our standards come from. 'When we grow up in a family, we often take on the parent voice and internalise it so that it becomes our internal voice: the voice of standards . . . If my parent voice says that whatever I do is never good enough, I will start believing that about myself. I may never realise that the voice is not my own, but that it actually belongs to my parents. But if we can recognise the source of that voice, we can ask, "What about me? Do I accept this? What about God? Does he accept my best? *Is my best good enough for God?" And of course it is.* His "parent voice" is a voice of grace, love and acceptance and is the only parent voice worth listening to. Most of us gain self-approval by living up to our own standards'[13] (my italics). The authors encourage us to pray: 'Father God, remind me that the only internal voice worth listening to is Yours; that You are "mighty to save" me from a lifetime cycle of low self-esteem.'[14]

The message is that we should disregard our parents' moral guidance because they set standards that are difficult to meet. But this is misleading advice, for the Bible instructs us to obey our parents. 'My son, *keep your father's command, and do not forsake the law of your mother*. Bind them continually upon your heart; tie them around your neck. When you roam, they will lead you; when you sleep, they will keep you; and when you awake, they will speak with you' *(Proverbs 6.20-22)*. Our parents give moral guidance because they love us and want what is best for us. Scripture instructs parents to bring their children up in the training and admonition of the Lord *(Ephesians 6.4)*. So when we are told to disregard our parents' voice, we are actually being encouraged to disobey Scripture. Indeed, self-esteem dogma positively encourages us *not* to listen to the voice of our parents, for the only voice worth listening to is that of the permissive god of the self-esteem movement, who always accepts our best. The amoral tone of this teaching is clear. The fifth commandment to honour our father and mother is ignored; the wisdom of Solomon is rejected.

The statement that *our best* is good enough for God is a distortion of the Gospel of grace. If *our best* is good enough for God, why did Christ die on the cross? Scripture teaches that all our righteousness is like filthy rags in the sight of God *(Isaiah 64.6)*. *Our best* is not good enough – we need the righteousness which is from God by faith in Christ.

The suggestion that we gain approval by living up to our own standards is anathema, for God's Word sets the standard by which Christians are commanded to live. 'Blessed are the undefiled in the way, who walk in the law of the Lord!' *(Psalm 119.1)*. The inner voice that lets us know when we do wrong is our conscience, which is reinforced by Scripture and by our parents' moral guidance. It is pagans who set their own moral standards, and do what is right in their own eyes.

(iii) Christians with a distorted image of God

The authors argue that for Christians, healthy self-esteem means having the right image of God. 'Our image, or images, of God – because sometimes we have many – are critically important to our spiritual well-being. If we have a distortion of who God is, we will not have a healthy estimate of ourselves as people.'[15] They continue, 'We need to get out of our predictable tracks of thinking, challenge and question the distorted images we have of God, and replace them with a clear and true image ... We need to do so because those distorted images of God actually affect our low self-esteem, which affects our distorted image of God and consequently our relationship with him: another negative cycle. An accurate image of God will increase our self-esteem and help us develop a good relationship with God.'[16]

The presupposition is that Christians struggle to acquire an accurate image of God. This demonstrates a poor understanding of the Gospel. Jesus Christ 'is the image of the invisible God' *(Colossians 1.15)* and the Spirit of Christ lives in the believer. 'Now if anyone does not have the Spirit of Christ, he is not His' *(Romans 8.9)*. A true believer cannot have a false image of God, for we know whom we have believed and are persuaded that he is able to keep that which we have committed to him against that Day *(2 Timothy 1.12)*. It is an unbeliever, not a Christian, who has suppressed the truth of God in unrighteousness, who has a false image of God. An idolater has distorted the image of God, not a man who is alive in Christ.

The authors assert that 'Bible verses which remind us of God's command to be obedient may cause guilt to arise ... We continually strive to please God, yet never feel that we have pleased him – our self-esteem tumbles down the ladder.'[17] We need to bring the right biblical image of God into our thought processes. We need to see God as a gracious and merciful Father who 'accepts us totally, exactly as we are'.[18]

The inference is that Christians should not focus on obedience to God's commands, for to do so causes our self-esteem to tumble. Therefore to preserve our self-esteem we should rather focus on God's grace which accepts us totally, exactly as we are. The statement that God 'accepts us totally, exactly as we are' ignores the truth that it is only in Christ that we are acceptable to God. And Christ said if we love him we will keep his commandments *(John 14.15)*. The man who says he is a Christian and 'does not keep His commandments, is a liar, and the truth is not in him' *(1 John 2.4)*.

Here we see a key feature of the self-esteem movement; it does not regard obedience to God's commands as all-important. Indeed, it even suggests that Jesus' commandment that we must obey him might cause Christians to have low self-esteem. The implication is that as God loves us unconditionally he doesn't really mind if we commit the odd sin or two. After all, God really wants to meet our needs, keep us happy and ensure that we feel good about ourselves. And if that means overlooking his rather high standards, so be it. So we are encouraged to believe that God accepts us exactly as we are, with all our sin and disobedience.

(iv) Christians must love themselves

The authors claim that God wants Christians to love themselves. 'As Christians we so often say that we love our neighbour but we don't finish the command. We say, "I love them and I will do anything for them, but I don't love me." It's important that we learn to love ourselves simply because God loves us.'[19] And so we must ask ourselves: 'How patient am I with myself, how kind am I to myself, how angry do I get with myself, do I protect myself, how easy do I find it to trust myself, do I value myself as God values me?'[20]

Here we see the focus of the self-esteem movement – it's all about *me*. I must trust myself, I must love myself, I must value myself for I am at the centre and God is out there somewhere, doing his best to keep me happy. But this is not the message of the Bible. Scripture teaches that it is natural for a man, created in the image of God, to love himself, 'for no one ever hated his own flesh' *(Ephesians 5.29)*. Self-esteem dogma wants us to have an excessive love for self, such that we become completely self-centered. Jesus has commanded those who follow him to deny themselves, to take up their cross and to follow him – the One who teaches us to put the needs of others above our own needs.

(v) Low self-esteem in John's Gospel

Insight into Self-esteem interprets the story of the woman at the well, from the fourth chapter of the *Gospel of John*, as the story of a woman with low self-esteem.[21] What the Bible forgot to tell us, according to the authors, is that the woman grew up with a sense of low self-esteem because she was 'desperate for the love and approval that her parents could not give. Her family life was dysfunctional and her relationship with her dad wasn't close. He often told her that she was no good; he never said "I love you."'[22] And her mother, worn down by the demands of marriage and children, had little to give her.

According to this psychological interpretation of *John 4*, her inner voice often called her 'unlovable'. As a result of her uncaring parents, 'the only way she knew how to feel valued was to give herself to men'. And so 'she ended up living an isolated and lonely life, a very needy woman, her low self-esteem affecting the way she lives, taking away her hope . . . Just as her self-esteem had hit rock bottom and she wondered how much longer she could go on, she met a man.'[23] Here was the man who would save her, not from sin but from low self-esteem.

Jesus gently took the cover off her life. 'The wounds were deep. Past hurts, past disappointments. She realised that he knew that she was living with a man whose love could not embrace her neediness to feel valued. Somehow, deep within her very being, beyond the hurt and pain, she knew that this man could do that . . . this man's love was different . . . This man Jesus totally accepted her. He accepted her despite her wounds, even because of them and gave her an assurance, a certainty of feeling valued for the first time in her life . . . Because now she mattered to someone who esteemed her for being a woman; for being herself . . . She felt valued, loved, held in high esteem, by the man who asked her for a drink – and who by doing so, had given her life.'[24]

CWR's interpretation of *John 4* shows how Scripture is twisted to support the teaching of the self-esteem movement. There is, of course, nothing in Scripture to say that the woman was mistreated by her parents – that is simple invention. There is nothing in Scripture to say that she had low self-esteem. CWR has added to Scripture to make it appear to support their false dogma of self-esteem.

Notice the heretical nature of CWR's teaching on self-esteem. According to *Insight*, the woman's main problem is her low self-esteem, not her sin. There is no understanding that she was a sinner in desperate need of salvation from sin. Jesus is presented as the One who came to save her from low self-esteem, not as the One who came to seek and save sinners. There is no suggestion that she needs to repent and place her faith in Christ, the Saviour of the world. Her need is to feel valued, not to obtain forgiveness and to be born again. According to CWR, salvation is through enhancing her self-esteem.

Insight into Self-esteem is simply regurgitating secular self-esteem dogma in the name of the Christian faith. Christians should not be deceived by this false teaching. As Christians we are required to live by God's standards. We have a God-given conscience that warns us when we do wrong. We are required to obey God's commands and to live a life worthy of the Gospel of Christ.

David Seamands, pioneer of the self-esteem movement

David Seamands is a big name in the Christian counselling movement, as we saw in chapter three. He specialises in the type of counselling known as healing of the memories.

His book *Healing for Damaged Emotions*, which has sold over a million copies and has been translated into over thirty languages, is a polemic in support of the dogma of self-esteem. The foreword by George Verwer of Operation Mobilisation is wholehearted in its praise. 'It is hard to express how excited I am about this book and the way I have seen the Lord use it . . . It is my prayer that you will not only prayerfully read this book, but also distribute copies to others.'[25] James Dobson is equally enthusiastic in his support: 'Dr Seamands is an unusually sensitive and insightful analyst of today's emotional stresses, especially as they relate to spiritual growth and understanding. I enthusiastically recommend this book to professionals and lay people.' There can be no doubt that the teaching of this book has been fully embraced and supported by mainstream evangelical Christianity.

(i) 'Healing for Damaged Emotions'

The central theme of *Healing for Damaged Emotions* is that real Christians need positive self-esteem. Seamands claims that low self-esteem is a weapon Satan uses to cause Christians to live defeated, miserable lives. 'They find themselves defeated by the most powerful psychological weapon that Satan uses against Christians. This weapon has the effectiveness of a deadly missile. Its name? Low self-esteem. Satan's greatest psychological weapon is a gut-level feeling of inferiority, inadequacy, and low self-worth. This feeling shackles many Christians.'[26] Low self-esteem can keep Christians marching around in vicious circles of fear and uselessness.[27] Scripture, however, teaches that Satan's deadliest weapon is deception, for he is the father of lies. The idea that low self-esteem is Satan's deadliest weapon comes from the imagination of Seamands.

(ii) The parable of the talents

Seamands uses the parable of the talents to illustrate the effect of low self-esteem. 'The man with the one talent was immobilised by fear and feelings of inadequacy. Because he was so afraid of failure he didn't invest his talent, but buried it in the ground and tried to play it safe . . . He did what a lot of people with low self-esteem do – nothing.'[28] According to Seamands the servant who was given one talent did nothing because he was suffering with low-self esteem. But the Bible says nothing about low-self esteem. His lord calls him a wicked and lazy servant who is to be cast into the outer darkness *(Matthew 25.26, 30)*. The text says that the wicked servant feared his lord – fear of failure is Seamands' addition to the text.

(iii) The Israelites and the Promised Land

Seamands says that the Israelites were afraid to occupy the Promised Land because of their low self-esteem. 'The dream was ready and God was ready, but the people weren't because of their low self-esteem. "We are grasshoppers." They forgot that they were children of God. They forgot who they were and what they were.'[29] On the basis of this story Seamands concludes, 'In our low self-esteem, we destroy God's dream for us as a community of believers – we who are his very own body. What happened to your dream? Where is the vision God put before you? What wrecked it? Your sins and transgressions and bad habits? I doubt it. Probably your dream has been delayed or destroyed because Satan tricked you into thinking of yourself as a grasshopper or a worm.'[30]

Scripture gives a different interpretation of this event. In their unbelief the Israelites rejected God and his prophet Moses, and wanted to elect another leader and return to Egypt. Moses confessed the great iniquity of the people and prayed that God, according to his great mercy, would pardon this terrible sin of unbelief. And the Lord said to Moses, 'How long shall I bear with this evil congregation who complain against Me? I have heard the complaints which the children of Israel make against Me' *(Numbers 14.27)*. All those who complained against God were condemned to die in the wilderness. Scripture does not mention self-esteem. The story is about Israel's rebellion and unbelief. It is not difficult to see that Scripture is being misused to make it say what it clearly does not say. Seamands has twisted Scripture in an attempt to provide biblical support for self-esteem dogma.

(iv) The three great commandments

In a further desperate attempt to support self-esteem dogma from Scripture, Seamands claims Christ commands us to love ourselves. 'The great commandment is that you love God with all your being. The second commandment is an extension of the first – that you love your neighbour as you love yourself. We do not have two commandments here, but three: to love God, to love yourself, and to love others. I put self second, because Jesus plainly made a proper self-love the basis of a proper love for neighbour. The term self-love has a wrong connotation for some people. Whether you call it self-esteem or self-worth, it is plainly the foundation of Christian love for others. And this is the opposite of what many Christians believe.'[31] Once again Seamands is misusing Scripture. Christ clearly taught that there were two commandments. It is incredible that Seamands should claim three commandments in a passage where Christ emphatically stated that there were two, and indicated that the second was like the first. Yet this verse is frequently cited to support the dogma of self-love. Significantly the Bible warns us that a feature of a false teacher is that he twists the Scriptures.

Seamands' final blow is to make the amazing generalisation that parents are one of the more important causes of low-self esteem. It is the 'messages they send to you about yourself through their facial expressions, tones, attitudes, words and actions'.[32]

James Dobson and Focus on the Family

At the centre of Dobson's soothing psychological advice is a deep commitment to the dogma of self-esteem. He makes the astounding claim that 'lack of self-esteem produces more symptoms of psychiatric disorders than any other factor yet identified'.[33] Dobson stresses the absolute importance of self-esteem as the central message of his ministry. 'If I could write a prescription for the women of the world, I would provide each one of them with a healthy dose of self-esteem and personal worth (taken three times a day until the symptoms disappear). I have no doubt that this is their greatest need.' [34] According to Dobson, the best kept secret of the year is that women feel inferior. To support this assertion he tells the story of an outwardly confident woman who came to him for counselling 'and wept for more than an hour as she tried to express the inexpressible anguish of inferiority'.[35] The inferiority complex that Dobson claims most women suffer leads to their low self-esteem.

Dobson goes even further in his claims about the epidemic of low self-esteem that is affecting America. Not only women, but a majority of Americans experience low self-esteem, and this has serious implications for the stability of American culture, 'because the health of an entire society depends on the ease with which its individual members can gain personal acceptance. Thus, whenever the keys to self-esteem are seemingly out of reach for a large percentage of the people, as in twentieth-century America, then widespread mental illness, neuroticism, hatred, alcoholism, drug abuse, violence, and social disorder will certainly occur. Personal worth is not something humans are free to take or leave. We must have it, and when it is unattainable, everybody suffers.'[36] This is amazing stuff, for Dobson is contradicting the teaching of Christ, who said that from within, out of the heart of man come murders, wickedness, pride and all manner of sin. The idea that the cause of violence, hatred and social disorder is low self-esteem is an idea not supported by Scripture.

Dobson sees low self-esteem as a universal curse, like original sin, that affects the whole of humanity. He writes that 'low self-esteem is a threat to the entire human family, affecting children, adolescents, the elderly, all socioeconomic levels of society, and each race and ethnic culture. It can engulf anyone who feels disrespected in the eyes of other people.'[37] In Dobson's gospel, low self-esteem has replaced sin as the cause of mankind's problem – for all have low self-esteem, and fall short of feeling good about themselves! His ministry is to save mankind from the curse of low self-esteem.

(i) Self-esteem for children

A search of the website of Focus on the Family elicited over a thousand references to self-esteem. The website reminds parents that adolescent girls, especially those with low self-esteem, may fall prey to a sudden increase in male attention. 'Parents should talk to their children about sexual behaviour before this point, as young people who develop healthy self-esteem early in life are typically better able to navigate the rough waters of adolescence.' This idea comes from secular sex education – it teaches that low self-esteem is one of the main causes of unwanted teenage pregnancies. Scripture does not teach that we should strive to enhance our children's self-esteem to protect them from moral danger, but that we should diligently teach them God's law (*Deuteronomy 6.7*).

Dobson advises parents to build their child's self-esteem through affirmation. 'Preteens need lots of support at home to avoid having their self-esteem stomped on as they enter adolescence. Follow these tips and help your child "ace" the middle years. Affirm, Affirm, and Affirm. Catch your children doing something right and praise them for it. Emphasise their positive qualities and behaviours. Be specific with your praise: "I appreciate you because . . .", "I was pleased to see you . . .", "Thank you for . . ." To appreciate means "to raise in value". Your verbal praise will raise your child's self-esteem. Likewise, constant criticism will lower it.' This advice is outrageously permissive and completely unbiblical. Parents have a duty to train their children in the discipline and instruction of the Lord.

(ii) The burden of low self-esteem

Dobson explains the burden of low self-esteem with these words. 'I would depict a bowed, weary traveller. Over his shoulder I would place the end of a mile-long chain to which is attached tons of scrap iron, old tyres, and garbage of all types. Each piece of junk is inscribed with the details of some humiliation – a failure – an embarrassment – a rejection from the past. He could let go of the chain and free himself from that heavy load which immobilises and exhausts him, but he is somehow convinced that it must be dragged throughout life. So he plods onward, digging a furrow in the good earth as he goes.'[38]

Dobson's description sounds very much like the burden of sin that Pilgrim bore before it was lifted at Calvary. This is highly significant because in Dobson's gospel, low self-esteem has taken the place of sin. Man needs salvation not from the chains of sin but from the chains of low self-esteem. Those who experience Dobson's message of salvation can sing with joy:

> *My chains fell off, my heart was free,*
> *Self-esteem is high, I live for me!*

In their book, *James Dobson's Gospel of Self-Esteem & Psychology,* Martin and Deidre Bobgan describe Dobson's tremendous influence in bringing psychology and self-esteem teachings into the church. While conceding that there are some pluses to Dobson's ministry (I have not found them), the Bobgans claim that 'many of his specific teachings actually originated from secular psychological theorists whose opinions are based on godless foundations. Thus, Dobson uses the Bible as a sanction for dispensing unbiblical ideas to unsuspecting readers and listeners. The use of psychology to help people eclipses the Scriptures at Focus on the Family. Self-esteem and psychology are the two major thrusts that too often supersede sin, salvation and sanctification. They are another gospel.'[39] The Bobgans could have added that Scripture warns that even if an angel from Heaven 'preaches any other gospel to you than what you have received, let him be accursed' *(Galatians 1.8).*

Summary of Christian self-esteem dogma

The following are the key points of the Christian version of self-esteem.

1. The central premise of Christian self-esteem dogma is that the purpose of the Gospel is to make us feel good about ourselves, to make us happy. There is no acceptance of suffering as part of the Christian life. 'For to you it has been granted on behalf of Christ, not only to believe in Him, but also to suffer for His sake' *(Philippians 1.29).*

2. The Christian counselling movement, following the wisdom of secular humanism, agrees that the greatest cause of social and behavioural problems is low self-esteem, not sin.

3. The Christian counselling movement blatantly misinterprets Scripture in an attempt to justify its promotion of self-esteem dogma in the Christian church.

4. The Christian counselling movement, following the lead of the secular self-esteem movement, describes the conscience pejoratively as our parents' voice, which sets absolute, inflexible moral standards that make us feel a failure, and contribute to our low self-esteem. In effect, we are told that we should not listen to our conscience.

5. An underlying thesis of the Christian self-esteem movement is that we gain self-approval, and therefore healthy self-esteem, 'by living up to our own standards'.[40] Doing our best is good enough for the god of self-esteem. The inference is that God's moral law is the major cause of low self-esteem.

6. Christians are to be taught to love themselves. There is a great emphasis on me and my needs. The most important thing in life is for me to feel good about myself and to be happy. Self-denial is never mentioned; discipline is unheard of.

Christian self-esteem teaching is taken straight from the ideas of secular psychology and is fundamentally unbiblical. It is a heretical teaching that has been introduced into the church by the Christian counselling movement and popular Christian leaders.

Self-esteem Dogma in the Light of Scripture

IN THE PREVIOUS TWO CHAPTERS we saw the secular explanation of self-esteem dogma and the false view propagated by the Christian counselling movement. We concluded that the Christian self-esteem movement has taken its message straight from the ideas of secular psychology and is fundamentally unbiblical. Now we must turn to Scripture in order to understand how many in the church are being misled.

Based in humanistic psychology

Scripture does not mention self-esteem – it is a term that has emerged from the humanist psychology of Maslow and Rogers. So we must understand that the dogma of self-esteem is entirely the construct of secular humanism. As such, it denies the spiritual dimension of life, does not accept the moral law of God, and certainly does not understand that God's law is written in the human heart - Romans 2:12-16). And more, it does not accept the fallen nature of man and does not recognise that an unregenerate man is a slave to sin. Instead, it sees

14

Self-esteem Dogma in the Light of Scripture

IN THE PREVIOUS TWO CHAPTERS we saw the secular explanation of self-esteem dogma and the false view propagated by the Christian counselling movement. We concluded that the Christian self-esteem movement has taken its message straight from the ideas of secular psychology and is fundamentally unbiblical. Now we must turn to Scripture in order to understand how many in the church are being misled.

Based in humanistic psychology

Scripture does not mention self-esteem – it is a term that has emerged from the humanist psychology of Maslow and Rogers. So we must understand that the dogma of self-esteem is entirely the construct of secular humanism. As such, it denies the spiritual dimension of life, does not accept the moral law of God, and certainly does not understand that God's law is written in the human heart *(Romans 2.12-16)*. And more, it does not accept the fallen nature of man and does not recognise that an unregenerate man is a slave to sin. Instead, it sees humans as essentially good, autonomous, needy individuals, who are continually seeking to meet their psychological needs for security, self-worth and significance. It therefore fails lamentably as an explanation of human behaviour.

Psychologists tell us that to even talk about sin upsets people and is bad for our self-esteem. Linleigh Roberts, director of Biblical Foundations, makes the point that many psychologists and psychiatrists 'have devised ways to avoid the problem [of sin] or at least to divert attention away from it; those who take a biblical approach and meet the problem head on are not popular, even in Christian circles.'[1] So it is no surprise that both humanist psychologists and the Christian counselling movement have chosen to replace the spiritual problem of sin with the psychological problem of low self-esteem. What is surprising is the large number of Christians who are happy to speak about low self-esteem but reluctant to talk about sin.

The Fall of man and self-esteem

The Fall of man, described in *Genesis 3*, helps us to understand the root of self-esteem dogma. In the Garden of Eden, after Adam and Eve had eaten the forbidden fruit, they felt ashamed, afraid, guilty and naked, and, covering themselves with fig leaves, they hid from God *(Genesis 3.7-10)*. A psychological interpretation of this event would describe Adam and Eve's profound feelings of shame, fear and guilt, and their action of covering themselves with fig leaves and hiding from God amongst the trees of the Garden, as evidence that eating the forbidden fruit had affected their self-esteem. And when God drove them out of the Garden, their self-esteem received a great blow. Indeed, this was surely human self-esteem at its lowest point. In the mind of self-esteem dogma, the cause of Adam and Eve's low self-esteem was the unreasonable, inflexible (you shall not eat of the tree of the knowledge of good and evil) command of God. So we see that the underlying cause of low self-esteem is the effect God's absolute moral law has on our conscience. The cure is to ignore the commands of God. After all, why should Adam and Eve feel guilty simply because they chose to eat the delicious fruit from one of the trees in the Garden?

Scripture, on the other hand, teaches that Adam and Eve felt ashamed, guilty and naked because they had sinned against God by disobeying his command. Their shame, guilt and nakedness was the consequence of their sin – they knew that they had disobeyed God and their conscience troubled them so much that they hid from God, even before God challenged them about their sin. And Adam and Eve could not even blame their parents for their rebellious conduct! Although Adam tried to blame Eve, and Eve the serpent, God made it clear that they were both responsible for their actions. Of their own free will they had chosen to disobey God. The cause of what self-esteem dogma has chosen to call low self-esteem is not our parents, or other people treating us badly, but disobedience to God's Word.

Our God-given conscience

Because God has placed his law in our hearts, and has given us a conscience to warn of wrongdoing, we know that certain acts are wrong. Self-esteem dogma correctly recognises the role of the conscience, or what it has chosen to call our inner voice, as a major factor in making us feel guilty and ashamed when we do wrong. It follows that our God-given conscience is a large problem for the self-esteem movement, for it is difficult to make sinful men or women feel good about themselves. This is why self-esteem dogma persuades us not to listen to our conscience, for to do so makes us feel bad and guilty. For the same reason it is intensely opposed to absolute moral rules, such as the Ten Commandments, and advises us to take no notice of the 'oughts', 'musts' and 'thou shalt nots' that we have learned from our parents and from the church.

The solution to mankind's problem

Secular psychology teaches that the solution to mankind's deep-seated problem is to enhance our self-esteem. The first step is to release us from 'oughts' and 'musts', thereby releasing us from our moral duties and obligations. We are persuaded to dismiss God's authority and replace it with our own. We are encouraged to believe that our feelings, preferences and options should be the guide to behaviour. If we feel like doing something, then it must be okay. We are persuaded to reject the idea of an absolute moral law as old-fashioned bigotry that nobody accepts anymore. All rules should be flexible, taking account of our circumstance and how we feel.

The next step in enhancing self-esteem is to convince us to feel good about ourselves, no matter how we behave. We are taught to accept ourselves irrespective of our sinful behaviour. And parents must affirm their children as acceptable and lovable, no matter how badly they behave. There must be no discipline, criticism or correction; we must not make our children feel that their behaviour has been wrong for that will damage their self-esteem. Discipline is another old-fashioned idea that is likely to cause self-esteem problems. The new way of self-esteem dogma is affirm, affirm, affirm, no matter how a child behaves.

The final step is for a sinful man to become self-actualised. Humanistic psychology teaches that humans have within themselves the potential to become truly fulfilled individuals who achieve happiness, meaning and purpose without God. So the real agenda of self-esteem dogma is to make a sinful man or woman feel good about their sin. We achieve healthy self-esteem when we ignore God's moral law, learn to enjoy sin, and feel good about it. In all that has been written and taught about self-esteem, both Christian and secular, there is never any suggestion that the root cause of man's low self-esteem is God's moral law which condemns sinful behaviour.

The biblical solution is to give a man a new heart, to make him a new man in Christ. On the cross Christ became sin for us so that we can be forgiven and set free from the bondage of sin. 'My chains [of sin] fell off, my heart was free [from slavery to sin], I rose, went forth and followed thee [Christ my Saviour]'. And the Saviour commands those who follow him to deny themselves, to take up their cross daily and follow him. Denial of self means *not* putting our interests first, but our commitment to Christ. Taking up our cross means being prepared to suffer for the sake of the Gospel. Jesus said 'whoever loses his life for My sake and the gospel's will save it' *(Mark 8.35)*. Self-sacrifice and self-denial are the way of Christ. The apostle Paul said, 'Nor do I count my life dear to myself, so that I may finish my race with joy, and the ministry which I received from the Lord Jesus' *(Acts 20.24)*.

The folly of the Christian self-esteem movement

We have seen self-esteem dogma take root in the fertile soil of humanistic psychology. The folly of the Christian self-esteem movement is that it has attempted to integrate the secular ideas of humanistic psychology with the Gospel of Christ. Those who propagate self-esteem dogma in the name of Christ are modern Gnostics who have built their theology upon the psychological theories of men. The Word of God has been diluted and manipulated to support psychological speculations. The Christian self-esteem movement is infiltrating the false ideas of godless men into the church.

A feature of Christian self-esteem dogma is its low view of sin. Indeed, it seldom uses the word for fear of damaging our fragile self-esteem. According to CWR, 'If our standards are so high as to be almost unobtainable we will put ourselves forward for failure.'[2] Absolute laws are inconvenient for we have difficulty meeting them and that makes us feel bad. The solution is for us to choose standards that are realistic and achievable. We must remember that as long as we do our best to live up to *our standards,* God is satisfied. CWR explains, 'Most of us gain self-approval by living up to our *own standards.*'[3]

The permissive god of 'Christian' self-esteem dogma longs to satisfy the needs and desires of the human heart. He delights in meeting our needs and likes to make us feel good about ourselves, no matter what. He is careful not to set standards too high or too difficult for us to meet. He is satisfied with our behaviour so long as we do our best. He is a god who is 'mighty to save' mankind from a lifetime cycle of low self-esteem. And if the truth were known, he does not really hate evil and sin all that much, for he accepts us totally, exactly as we are. He has commanded us to love ourselves and he loves everybody unconditionally no matter how they behave.

What is the true biblical response to the issue of low self-esteem? As Christians we cannot accept the dogma of self-esteem, and therefore we must not accept the psychological label of low self-esteem. Indeed, to accept the label is to tacitly support the false teaching of secular humanism and the Christian counselling movement. Christians must not fall prey to the cult of self-worship that is now engulfing Western society. It is wrong for Christians to join the self-esteem bandwagon for it leads people away from the Gospel of Christ.

The Bible describes the status of a Christian in many ways. A Christian is a new man in Christ. He has been chosen in Christ before the foundation of the world, to be holy and without blame before God. He is a forgiven sinner, redeemed with the precious blood of Christ. He is an adopted son of God. 'Behold what manner of love the Father has bestowed on us, that we should be called children of God! ... Beloved, now we are children of God; and it has not yet been revealed what we shall be, but we know that when He is revealed, we shall be like Him' *(1 John 3.1, 2)*. A Christian is sealed with the Holy Spirit whereby he has access into the presence of God his Father. He is a disciple of Jesus Christ. He is a soldier in the army of Christ; he is a servant of his Master. A Christian is esteemed by God, because he is in Christ, the King of Glory. He is a member of a chosen generation, a royal priesthood, a holy nation. His purpose is to declare the praises of Christ who called him out of darkness into his marvellous light *(1 Peter 2.9)*. According to the apostle Paul, we are more than conquerors through him who loved us *(Romans 8.37)*.

A key message of Paul's letter to the *Philippians* is that we should have the same mindset as Christ – we should be like-minded, for Christ is our example. The attitude of Christ was one of humility. Although he is divine, the Second Person of the glorious Godhead, he did not regard equality with God something to be grasped, but humbled himself when he took on human flesh. He made himself of no reputation, and humbled himself to take on the role of a servant. He demonstrated his humility when he washed his disciples' feet, setting us an example. And Jesus went even further when he humbled himself to a shameful death on a cross. In obedience to God his Father, Christ endured the humility of the cross, to accomplish God's gracious plan of salvation. He commands his disciples to be like-minded. 'Therefore, as the elect of God, holy and beloved, put on tender mercies, kindness, humility, meekness, longsuffering' *(Colossians 3.12)*. In lowliness of mind we should esteem others better than ourselves. We should look out not for our own interests but for the interests of others *(Philippians 2.4)*.

Christ was humble and encouraged his disciples to be lowly in mind. Because we have the mind of Christ, we too are to be humble, to esteem others and to look to their interests and not our own. A true disciple of Christ does not seek his own self-esteem. In his final public sermon Jesus taught his disciples that 'he who loves his life will lose it, and he who hates his life in this world will keep it for eternal life' *(John 12.25)*. Those who follow Jesus do not spend time learning to love them-selves. The idea that a Christian should strive for healthy self-esteem is contrary to the teaching of Christ. The teaching of the Christian counselling movement that I should be kind to myself, protect myself, think highly of myself, trust myself, is to put *me* at the centre. I become self-centred, focused on myself. This is not the mind of Christ; this is anathema to the Christian faith.

God the Father has highly exalted the humble Christ, and given him a name that is above every name, that at the name of Jesus, every knee should bow. So the Lord Jesus did not exalt himself, but was exalted by his Father. In the same way a humble disciple of Christ will never seek his own self-esteem, for he is, and he will be, exalted and esteemed in Jesus Christ his Lord. When Christ is revealed we shall be like him, for we shall see him as he is. This is true esteem in the eyes of God our Father. Christ in me, the hope of glory.

15
Concluding Remarks

WE SET OUT in this book to examine two questions. Is counselling, as practised by the Christian counselling movement, a legitimate part of Christian ministry? And does the church benefit from integrating 'psychological truth' and Scripture? Those who promote Christian counselling claim that integrating biblical truth with psychological truth leads to a better understanding of the human condition, and a better understanding of how to help those suffering from inner hurts, depression and emotional problems. We have examined the ideas and assumptions that lie behind the Christian counselling scene and explored the flawed arguments for integrating Scripture and psychology. In doing so we have exposed the secular, godless roots from which Christian counselling has emerged and revealed the false ideas behind self-esteem dogma.

The dark side of Christian counselling

The Christian struggle is against the rulers of the darkness of this age, against spiritual hosts of wickedness in the heavenly places (*Ephesians 6.12*). Therefore Christians are warned to give no opportunity to the devil *(Ephesians 4.27)*, the great deceiver. His is a kingdom of darkness. Although Satan is the prince of darkness, he successfully presents himself as an angel of light *(2 Corinthians 11.14)*. God's special people have been called out of darkness into Christ's marvellous light *(1 Peter 2.9)*. So as children of light we must 'have no fellowship with the unfruitful works of darkness, but rather expose them' *(Ephesians 5.11)*.

We have unveiled the dark side of the Christian counselling movement, which is built on the foundation laid by the giants of psychotherapy. We have examined the foolish speculations that have come from the darkened minds of these godless men. Freud's idea of the unconscious is used to explain that people suffer from depression because of suppressed anger against their parents. Adler's idea of a 'fictional' final goal has supposedly helped Christian counsellors understand human behaviour. Rogers' non-directive counselling has been accepted uncritically by Christian counsellors as the best way to help women decide whether or not to have an abortion. Ellis' Rational Emotive Behaviour Therapy, which undermines biblical absolutes, is used to help people with eating disorders. Maslow's theory persuades people that they need healthy self-esteem in order to feel significant and secure. Yet the teachings of these men are pure folly, for they walked 'in the futility of their mind, having their understanding darkened, being alienated from the life of God, because of the ignorance that is in them, because of the blindness of their heart' *(Ephesians 4.17-18)*.

More than the Gospel of grace

Behind the Christian counselling movement is a mindset that longs for more than is revealed in the Christian Gospel. We have heard Larry Crabb's claim that Christians need psychoanalysis to identify the sin that lies hidden below the waterline in their unconscious mind. According to Crabb, Christians need more than is on offer from tired clichés about the power of God and his Word. He wants the church to adopt a counselling model that facilitates the profound change that Christians really need. He teaches that Christian counselling will lead to a tremendous increase in spiritual and emotional maturity in our churches (see page 104).

The heart of Christian counselling has 'returned to Egypt', for it is no longer satisfied with the Gospel of grace. Just as the Israelites on their journey to the Promised Land longed for the fleshpots of Egypt, so the counselling movement longs for the seductive teachings that have come from the world of psychology. Indeed, psychological therapies have become so accepted by contemporary Christian thinking that they are considered to be a part of the faith.

Integrating Scripture with psychological theories

The evil of the integration model is that it has mixed God's truth with ungodly ideas. The integrationists' passion for the foolish theories of secular psychotherapy shows that they are striving to serve two masters. Their heart is divided between Christ and the giants of psychotherapy; they love their psychotherapeutic techniques more than they love the Word of God. They have brought the philosophy of the world into the Gospel of Christ – they have made the church a friend of the world. The doctrine of integration has seriously compromised the holiness and separateness of God's people.

The sufficiency of Scripture

While the Christian counselling movement pays lip service to Scripture, by its teaching and practice it undermines belief in the sufficiency of Scripture for all that pertains to life and godliness. We are told that Scripture is alright as far as it goes, but Christians need more than Scripture to deal with the difficult problems of daily living. It follows that Christians should not be denied the benefits that flow from psychological wisdom. On the basis of this reasoning many churches have a counselling ministry and virtually every theological college a course in pastoral care that teaches psychological theory.

False teaching

Combining Scripture with psychological theory has produced a false gospel. The greatest threat to God's people throughout the ages has come from those who claim to speak in God's name but are false prophets. While pretending to communicate the revealed truth of God, false teachers speak a deceptive lie and twist God's Word. False doctrine always manifests itself in wrong conduct. We have seen this in the self-esteem movement that has placed man at the centre, and God somewhere out there, longing to make us feel good about ourselves.

People now hope that the elevation of self-esteem will help them to overcome their spiritual problems. But this is a forlorn hope, for it denies the sinful nature of man and leads people away from the Cross of Christ.

A companion study in doctrine and conduct

We must recognise that the flawed beliefs of the Christian counselling movement affect both the doctrine and conduct of the church. The psychological approach has influenced the way Christians view God's love and the new concept of unconditional love has gained a great deal of credence. There has also been a change in the way many Christians view forgiveness. It is widely believed that Christians must forgive all who offend against them no matter what. Psychological thinking has also had a large impact on the way Christians deal with the problems of daily living, such as anxiety and depression. Here we should take note that the Christian counselling movement spends most of its time, and receives most of its income, from providing psychotherapy to people suffering with depression. A companion volume to this book will deal with the doctrinal issues mentioned above and seek to explain the difference between the psycho-secular view of depression, developed by the world of psychiatry, and what the Bible has to say about the issue.

From the evidence that we have uncovered, there can be no doubt that such Christian counselling is not a legitimate part of Christian ministry but an imposter that is misleading the church. We have come face to face with false teaching that has slipped into the church. We are led to the inevitable conclusion that the Christian counselling movement, which is propagating false teaching, poses a serious threat to the church and the Gospel.

Notes

Chapter 1

1 Clyde Narramore, *The Psychology of Counselling*, Zondervan, 1960, p11
2 Ibid., p12
3 Pastor Steven J. Cole, 'How John Calvin Led me to Repent of Christian Psychology', posted on 05/04/2005
4 Ibid.
5 Jay E. Adams, *Competent to Counsel*, Zondervan Publishing House, 1970, p17
6 Ibid., p82
7 *Christianity Today*, 2 October 1992, p28, cited from 'How John Calvin Led me to Repent of Christian Psychology' by Pastor Steven J. Cole
8 John D. Carter and Bruce Narramore, *The Integration of Psychology and Theology*, Rosemead Psychology Series, 1979, p9
9 The American Association of Christian Counsellors website, endorsements
10 www.psychoheresy-aware.org/ministry.html
11 Rick Warren, *Purpose Driven Church*, Grand Rapids, MI: Zondervan, 1995, p197
12 Ibid., pp219 & 225
13 Walter Chantry, *Today's Gospel – authentic or synthetic?* The Banner of Truth, first published 1970, reprinted 2007, p64
14 David F. Wells, *Losing our Virtue*, Inter-varsity Press, 1998, p42
15 Emmanuel Church Wimbledon, Newsletter, The Marriage Course, July/August 2008

Chapter 2

1 Selwyn Hughes, *My Story*, CWR, 2004, p219
2 Ibid., p263
3 Ibid., p293
4 Selwyn Hughes, *Christ Empowered Living*, Foreword by Larry Crabb, UK edition, 2005, CWR, p2
5 CWR website, seminars and courses, care and counselling
6 London School of Theology, Undergraduate Prospectus, 2007
7 Watford Christian Counselling Service website, affiliations, London School of Theology
8 Association of Christian Counselling website, mission statement, Christian counselling
9 Spurgeon's College website
10 Churches' Ministerial Counselling Service website
11 All Souls website
12 *Evangelicals Now*, 'Depression industry' by Nancy Lambrechts, July 2008

Chapter 3

1 Kirsten Birkett, *The Essence of Psychology*, 1999, Matthias Media, pp77-78
2 Frank Minirth and Paul Meier, *Happiness is a Choice*, Fleming H. Revell, 1994, p98
3 Paul Meier website, Christian counselling: what can I expect?
4 Selwyn Hughes, *Christ Empowered Living*, p11

5   Ibid., p239
6   Ibid., p125
7   Ibid., p109
8   Ibid., p113
9   Ibid., p145
10 Ibid., pp148-149
11 Ibid., p235
12 Ibid., pp152-153
13 David Seamands, *Healing for
    Damaged Emotions*, Authentic Media,
    edn 2006, p2
14 Ibid., Preface
15 Ibid., Preface
16 Ibid., p4
17 Ibid., pp3-4
18 Ibid., p6
19 Ibid., p7
20 Ibid., p46
21 Ibid., p13
22 Ibid., pp65-66
23 Ibid., p89
24 Agape Press, 'Pastor Concerned Over
    Fallout From Kentucky Minister's
    Moral Breach', by Jim Brown and
    Jenni Parker, August 10, 2005
25 Larry Crabb, *Understanding People*,
    Grand Rapids: Zondervan, 1987, p9
26 Ibid., p10
27 Ibid., p142
28 Ibid., p144
29 Ibid., p144
30 Larry Crabb, *Inside Out*, Navpress
    Publishing Group, 1988, p37
31 Ibid., p48
32 Ibid., p62
33 Ibid., p48
34 Ibid., p66
35 Ibid., p73
36 Ibid., p75
37 Gary Collins, *Christian Counselling:
    A comprehensive guide*, W Publishing
    Group, 1988, p22
38 Ibid., p22
39 James Dobson, *Hide or Seek, How
    To Build Self-Esteem in Your Child*,
    Fleming H. Revell, 1974, p21
40 James Dobson, *What Wives Wish
    their Husbands Knew about Women*,
    Tyndale House Publishers, 1975, p24

Chapter 4

1   John D. Carter and Bruce Narramore,
    *The Integration of Psychology and
    Theology*, Rosemead Psychology
    Series, 1979, p12
2   Ibid., p13
3   Ibid., p13
4   Ibid., p103
5   Fuller Seminary website
6   London School of Theology website,
    Theology & Counselling, What we
    believe about counselling
7   Watford Christian Counselling
    Service website
8   Larry Crabb, *Effective Biblical
    Counselling*, Zondervan, 1977, p47
9   Ibid., p56
10 Ibid., p44
11 Ibid., p96
12 Meier Clinics website
13 *Evangelicals Now*, 'Depression: how
    churches and GPs can work together',
    by Dr Mike Davies and Charles H.
    Whitworth, October 2008

Chapter 5

1   Larry Crabb, *Understanding People*,
    Grand Rapids: Zondervan, 1987,
    pp215-216
2   Selwyn Hughes, *Christ Empowered
    Living*, p149
3   Ibid., p126
4   Frank Minirth and Paul Meier,
    Happiness is a Choice, Fleming H.
    Revell, 1994, p97
5   Ibid., p97
6   Sigmund Freud, Standard Edition
    (SE) XX, *An Autobiographical Study*,
    Hogarth Press, London, 1968, p60
7   Ibid., p8
8   J. N. Isbister, *Freud – An Introduction
    to his Life and Work*, Polity Press,
    1985, p191
9   Paul Vitz, *Sigmund Freud's Christian
    Unconscious*, The Guilford Press,
    p110

10 David Bakan, *Sigmund Freud and the Jewish Mystical Tradition*, Beacon Press, 1975 edition, pp134-35
11 Ibid., p181
12 The first two have been provided by Velikovsky (1941) and Bakan (1958). Velikovsky, E. (1941), 'The dreams Freud dreamed', *Psychoanalytic Review*, 30, pp487-511.
13 Paul Vitz, *Sigmund Freud's Christian Unconscious*, p113
14 Eissler, K. R. (1971), *Talent and genius: The fictitious case of Tausk contra Freud*. New York: Quadrangle.
15 Paul Vitz, *Sigmund Freud's Christian Unconscious*, p128
16 Ibid., p165
17 Nicholas Sombart, Max Weber and Otto Gross, *History of Political Thought* 8 (1), Spring 1987, pp140-141
18 The Internet Encyclopaedia of Philosophy website, Sigmund Freud (1856-1939)
19 Frederick Crews, *The Memory Wars*, Granta Books, 1995, p9
20 Ibid., p110
21 Ibid., p298
22 Ibid., p298
23 Letter to Fliess, 19 September 1901, no. 146, *The Origins of Psycho-Analysis: Letters to Wilhelm Fliess, Drafts and Notes 1887-1902*, Basic Books, 1954, pp335-36
24 J. N. Isbister, *Freud – An Introduction to his Life and Work*, p178
25 Ibid., pp179-180

Chapter 6

1 Selwyn Hughes, *Christ Empowered Living*, p125
2 Ibid., pp125-127
3 Paul Brians, Department of English, Washington State University, website, The influence of Nietzsche
4 From a new translation of 'Individual Psychology, its Premises and Results' in *The Practice and Theory of Individual Psychology*,

   by Alfred Adler, in the AAISF/ATP Archives. Abstract from Adlerian website
5 Dr Henry Stein, 'Classical Adlerian Theory and Practice', a chapter in *Psychoanalytic Versions of the Human Condition: Philosophies of Life and Their Impact on Practice*, edited by Paul Marcus and Alan Rosenberg, 1998, New York University Press
6 Website of Alfred Adler Institute, Dr Henry Stein, Questions and answers

Chapter 7

1 Abraham Maslow, *Religions, Values, and Peak-Experiences*, Harmondsworth: Penguin, 1976 preface
2 Larry Crabb, *Effective Biblical Counselling*, Zondervan, 1977, p79
3 Ibid., p81
4 Maslow, *Religions, Values, and Peak-Experiences*, Chapter 8, Conclusions
5 Maslow, *Toward a Psychology of Being*, D. Van Nostrand Co., Princeton, N.J., 1962, p4
6 Ibid., p170
7 Maslow, *Toward a Psychology of Being* (1955-1957), Introduction: Toward a Psychology of Health, 1956
8 Maslow, *Motivation and Personality*, Harper & Row, 1970, p122
9 Maslow, *Toward a Psychology of Being*, p165
10 Maslow, *Motivation and Personality*, p117
11 Maslow, *A Theory of Human Motivation*, 1943, originally published in *Psychological Review*, 50, pp370-396
12 Maslow, *Toward a Psychology of Being*, p27
13 Maslow, *Emotional Literacy and Ortho-Education, How to Make the World a Better Place*, Chapter 6
14 Maslow, *A Theory of Human Motivation*, p382
15 Ibid., p383

16 Ibid., Chapter 7, Hypertext Meanings and Commentaries by Mark Zimmerman
17 Maslow, *Religions, Values and Peak-Experiences*, p20
18 Ibid., p45
19 Raylene Chang, 'Characteristics of the self-actualized person; Visions from the East and West', *Counselling & Values*: vol. 36, no. 1, October 1991, pp2-10
20 Maslow, *Toward a Psychology of Being*, p165
21 *Maslow's Hierarchy, How the House of Cards Crumbles*, Christian Discernment Publications Ministry, p31

Chapter 8

1 Larry Crabb, *Effective Biblical Counselling*, Zondervan Publishing House, 1977, p96
2 Selwyn Hughes, *Christ Empowered Living*, p246
3 Rogers, Carl Ransom, Introduction: Psychologists and their Theories, Enotes.com
4 Carl R. Rogers, *On Becoming a Person*, Houghton Mifflin, 1961, p135f, cited from *Psychology as Religion: the cult of self-worship* by Paul Vitz, Eerdmans Publishing, 1977, p22
5 Ibid., p139f
6 Ibid., p34
7 Ibid., p119
8 Dr C. G. Boeree, An Essay on Carl Rogers
9 Rogers, *On Becoming a Person*, pp23-24
10 Ibid., p27
11 Ibid., p194
12 Ibid., p91
13 Ibid., p35
14 Ibid., p189
15 Experiments in Moral Education by William Kilpatrick, Boston College, PWPA/ICUS Evening Speaker, Identity and Character, The Seventh International Congress of Professors World Peace Academy, Washington

Hilton and Towers Washington D.C., USA, November 24-29, 1997, WCSF III Official Event
16 Ibid.
17 Allan Guttmacher Report on Public Policy, Vol 7 Number 3, August 2004
18 The article *How Directional is Non-directional counselling?* (LIFE News Issue 52)
19 Rogers, *A Way of Being*, Houghton Mifflin, 1980, p83
20 Ibid., p90
21 Ibid., p90
22 Ibid., p91

Chapter 9

1 Website of the Albert Ellis Institute
2 Selwyn Hughes, *Christ Empowered Living*, p238
3 Ibid., p239
4 Helena Wilkinson, *Insight into Eating Disorders*, Waverley Abbey Insight Series, CWR, p87
5 Ibid., pp88-89
6 Ibid., p91
7 Ibid., p92
8 From Utne Reader, March-April 1997, p72 (Sidebar to The Greatest Story Never Told: Researcher Dave Larson says that finding God can improve your health and he has the numbers to prove it. So why aren't more people listening?)
9 Albert Ellis, *Are Capitalism, Objectivism, Libertarianism Religions?* Walden Three, 2006, Chapter 5, Assorted Evils of Ayn Rand's Objectivism, online
10 Ellis, *Reason and Emotion in Psychotherapy*, revised and updated. New York: Carol Publishing Group, 1994, pp292-293
11 Ellis, *Are Capitalism, Objectivism, Libertarianism Religions?* Walden Three, 2006, Chapter 6, Assorted Evils of Ayn Rand's Objectivism, online
12 Ellis, *The Case Against Religion*, American Atheist Press, p2

13 Ibid., p18
14 Ibid., p23
15 Ellis, *Reason and Emotion in Psychotherapy*, Citadel Press, 1977, pp321-322
16 Ibid., p125
17 Ibid., p137
18 Ellis, *The Case Against Religion*, p17
19 Ibid., p15
20 An Interview with Albert Ellis, PhD, by Myrtle Heery, http://www.psycho-therapy.net/interview/Albert_Ellis
21 Ellis, *Reason and Emotion in Psychotherapy*, p406
22 Ibid., p129
23 Ellis, *Is Objectivism a Religion?* Chapter 6, Why Objectivism is a Fanatical Religion, Lyle Stuart, New York, complete book online.
24 Ibid., Chapter 6, online
25 Ellis, *Are Capitalism, Objectivism, Libertarianism Religions?* Walden Three, 2006, Chapter 6, Why objec-tivism is a fanatical religion, p15 online
26 Ellis, *Is Objectivism a Religion?* Chapter 5, Assorted Evils of Ayn Rand's Objectivism, online, cited (Ellis, 1958, 2002b, 2003b; Ellis & Blau, 1998)
27 Ellis, *Reason and Emotion in Psychotherapy*, p183
28 Ellis, *Is Objectivism a Religion?* Chapter 15, Summary and Conclusions, online
29 Stevan L. Nielsen, W. Brad Johnson, Albert Ellis, *Counselling and Psychotherapy with Religious Persons: A Rational Emotive Behaviour Approach*, Lawrence Erlbaum Associates, 2001, p3
30 New York, News and Features, 11/07/2005, Behaviorists Behaving Badly, Does Albert Ellis – elderly sexologist and godfather of cognitive psychotherapy – really deserve to be banished from the Upper East Side institute that bears his name? By Matt Dobkin

Chapter 10

1 Abraham Maslow, *Toward a Psychology of Being*, p4
2 Albert Ellis, *The Case Against Religion*, American Atheist Press, p2
3 Ibid., p18
4 Ibid., p15
5 David Seamands, *Healing for Damaged Emotions*, Authentic Media, edition 2006, p2
6 Ruth Graham McIntire, *Youthworker*, May/June 2000, p25

Chapter 11

1 Martin and Deidre Bobgan, *Larry Crabb's Gospel*, EastGate Publishers, 1998, pp6-7
2 Ibid., p28
3 Larry Crabb, *Effective Biblical Counselling*, Zondervan, 1977, pp46-47
4 Ibid., p47
5 Ibid., p48
6 Ibid., pp51-52
7 Ibid., p61
8 Ibid., p69
9 Ibid., p77
10 Ibid., p76
11 Ibid., pp79-80
12 Ibid., p82
13 Ibid., p84
14 Crabb, *Understanding People*, Zondervan, 1987, p59
15 Ibid., p61
16 Ibid., p61
17 Crabb, *Effective Biblical Counselling*, p91
18 Ibid., p91
19 W. E. Vine, *Vine's Expository Dictionary*, Nelson, pp741-742
20 William Hendriksen, *Romans*, Bale Academic, p248
21 Crabb, *Understanding People*, pp142-43
22 Ibid., p143
23 Ibid., p129
24 Crabb, *Inside Out*, Navpress Publishing Group, 1988, p32
25 Ibid., p44

26 Crabb, *Understanding People*, p144
27 Ibid., p129
28 Ibid., p144
29 Ibid., p67
30 Ibid., p68
31 Ibid., p69
32 Crabb, *Inside Out*, p89
33 Ibid., pp82-83
34 Ibid., p100
35 Ibid., p103
36 Ibid., pp104-105
37 Ibid., p106
38 Ibid., p107
39 Crabb, *Understanding People*, p79
40 Ibid., p79
41 Crabb, *Effective Biblical Counselling*, p14
42 Ibid., p15
43 Crabb, *Finding God*, Zondervan, 1993, p99
44 Ibid., p104
45 Crabb, *Inside Out*, p114
46 Ibid., p115
47 Ibid., p99
48 Ibid., p100
49 Ibid., p120
50 Crabb, *Finding God*, p154
51 Ibid., p155
52 Ibid., pp155-156
53 Ibid., p156
54 Ibid., p156
55 Ibid., p157
56 Ibid., p158
57 *Evangelicals Now*, July 2006, Melvin Tinker's review of *The Pressure's Off*

Chapter 12

1 Nathaniel Branden, Our urgent need for self-esteem, article from website, originally published in Excellence 14/5/1994
2 California Task Force to Promote Self-Esteem and Personal and Social Responsibility, 1990, p4
3 National Association for Self-Esteem website
4 Ibid., Letter from the President, March 2004
5 *The Guardian*, 27 February 2007, Kathryn Ecclestone, All in the mind
6 *Myths & Reality: Teenage Pregnancy and Parenthood*, Report of the Teenage Parenthood Working Group
7 Abraham Maslow, *A Theory of Human Motivation*, p383
8 Abraham Maslow, *Towards a Psychology of Being*, Van Nostrand Reinhold, New York, p5
9 Douglas Groothuis, *Unmasking the New Age*, Intervarsity Press, 1986, p78
10 Melanie Fennell, *Overcoming Low Self-Esteem*, Robinson, 2001, p25
11 Ibid., p26
12 Ibid., p28
13 Ibid., p38
14 Ibid., p92
15 Ibid., p157
16 Ibid., p158
17 Ibid., p156
18 Ibid., p163
19 Ibid., p163
20 Ibid., p133
21 Ibid., p164

Chapter 13

1 James Dobson, *The New Hide and Seek*, Fleming H. Revell, third reprint 2003, p75
2 Robert Schuller, *Self-Esteem: The New Reformation*, Word Books, 1982
3 Ibid., p14
4 Joyce Meyer Ministries website, Is That Your Dripping Towel? by Joyce Meyer
5 *Look Great, Feel Great*, product description, ww.clcbookshops.com
6 Max Lucado, *Travelling Light: Releasing the burdens you were never intended to bear*, Nashville: W Publishing Group, 2001, p75
7 Oasis Trust website, training, self-esteem
8 Paul Vitz, *Psychology as Religion: The cult of self-worship*, William B. Eerdmans Publishing, 1977, p105
9 Chris Ledger and Wendy Bray, *Insight into Self-Esteem*, Waverley Abbey Insight Series, CWR, Surrey, 2006, p12
10 Ibid., p15

11 Ibid., pp28-29
12 Ibid., p43
13 Ibid., pp43-44
14 Ibid., p52
15 Ibid., p54
16 Ibid., p55
17 Ibid., p56
18 Ibid., p57
19 Ibid., p88
20 Ibid., p88
21 Ibid., p93
22 Ibid., p93
23 Ibid., p94
24 Ibid., pp96-97
25 David Seamands, *Healing for Damaged Emotions*, Authentic, foreword
26 Ibid., p46
27 Ibid., p54
28 Ibid., pp47-48
29 Ibid., p50
30 Ibid., p50
31 Ibid., p72
32 Ibid., p60
33 James Dobson, *Confident, Healthy Families*, Kingsway, 1987, pp73-74
34 James Dobson, *What Wives Wish their Husbands Knew about Women*, p35
35 Ibid., p36
36 Dobson, *Confident, Healthy Families*, p67
37 Dobson, *What Wives Wish their Husbands Knew about Women*, p24
38 Dobson, *Confident, Healthy Families*, p75
39 Martin and Deidre Bobgan, *James Dobson's Gospel of Self-Esteem & Psychology*, EastGate Publishers, 1990, pp8-9
40 Ibid., pp43-44

Chapter 14

1 Linleigh J. Roberts, *Let Us Make Man*, Banner of Truth, reprint 2001, p17
2 Chris Ledger and Wendy Bray, *Insight into Self-Esteem*, Waverley Abbey Insight Series, CWR, Surrey, 2006, p43
3 Ibid., p5

What is Going on in Christian Crisis Pregnancy Counselling?
E. S. Williams

91 pages, paperback. ISBN 978 1 870855 45 7

We hear of very many expectant mothers seeking abortion advice, including girls under sixteen. Dr Ted Williams, a medical doctor of long experience, and a noted specialist in the public health field, shows that Christian counselling centres have adopted a deeply compromised approach which provides non-judgemental advice that leaves in place the option of abortion.

Expectant mothers, including so many girls, should always be helped in a spirit of great compassion, but they must be advised according to the Book of God, and its eternal values.

This book will not only inform and warn, but will form the aims of pastors and all other Christians when they are called upon to extend help to expectant mothers thinking about abortion.

Faith, Doubts, Trials and Assurance
Peter Masters

176 pages, paperback. ISBN 978 1 870855 50 1

Obtaining faith is essential for answered prayer, all true worship, spiritual stability and real communion with God. In this book many questions are answered about faith, such as –

How may we assess the state of our faith?
How can faith be strengthened?
What are the most dangerous doubts?
How should difficult doubts be handled?
What is the biblical attitude to trials?
How can we tell if troubles are intended to chasten or to refine?
What can be done to obtain assurance?
What are the sources of assurance?
Can a believer commit the unpardonable sin?
Exactly how is the Lord's presence felt?

Dr Masters provides answers, with much pastoral advice, drawing on scripture throughout.

What is Going on in Christian Crisis Pregnancy Counselling?
E. S. Williams
91 pages, paperback, ISBN 978 1 870855 45 7

We hear of very many expectant mothers seeking abortion advice, including girls under sixteen. Dr Ted Williams, a medical doctor of long experience, and a noted specialist in the public health field, shows that Christian counselling centres have adopted a deeply compromised approach which provides non-judgemental advice that leaves in place the option of abortion.

Expectant mothers, including so many girls, should always be helped in a spirit of great compassion, but they must be advised according to the Book of God, and its eternal values.

This book will not only inform and warn, but will focus the aims of pastors and all other Christians when they are called upon to extend help to expectant mothers thinking about abortion.

Faith, Doubts, Trials and Assurance
Peter Masters
139 pages, paperback, ISBN 978 1 870855 50 1

Ongoing faith is essential for answered prayer, effective service, spiritual stability and real communion with God. In this book many questions are answered about faith, such as –

How may we assess the state of our faith?
How can faith be strengthened?
What are the most dangerous doubts?
How should difficult doubts be handled?
What is the biblical attitude to trials?
How can we tell if troubles are intended to chastise or to refine?
What can be done to obtain assurance?
What are the sources of assurance?
Can a believer commit the unpardonable sin?
Exactly how is the Lord's presence felt?

Dr Masters provides answers, with much pastoral advice, drawing on Scripture throughout.

Steps for Guidance in the Journey of Life
Peter Masters
134 pages, paperback, ISBN 978 1 870855 66 2

In recent years the subject of how to find God's guidance has become controversial. Some say that God does not have a specific plan for the lives of his people, but allows us to please ourselves. Others say God's will is known by dreams, visions, and 'words of knowledge'.

By contrast with these sadly unbiblical ideas, this book presents the time-honoured, scriptural view that Christians must seek God's will in all the major decisions of life, such as career, marriage, location, and church. Six essential steps are traced from the Bible, and principles are given on additional practical issues such as possessions and leisure activities; ambition and wealth; joining or leaving a church.

Here is a strong challenge to authentic Christian commitment, with an abundance of pastoral advice.

The Faith
Great Christian Truths
Peter Masters
119 pages, paperback, ISBN 978 1 870855 54 9

There is nothing like this popular, non-technical sweep through key themes of the Christian faith, highlighting very many inspiring and enlivening points. It often takes an unusual approach to a topic in order to bring out the full wonder and significance. It is designed to be enjoyed by seasoned Christians, and also by all who want to explore the great features of the faith, and discover the life of the soul.

CONTENTS:

The Mysterious Nature of a Soul	The New Birth
What God is Actually Like	Why the Resurrection?
The Fall of Man	Prophecies of Resurrection
The Three Dark Hours of Calvary	The Holy Trinity

Church Membership in the Bible
Peter Masters
61 pages, paperback, ISBN 978 1 870855 64 8

Christ has designed a 'home' or family for his people, described in these pages as an accomplishment of divine genius. This is a magnificent subject, vital to spiritual growth and blessing and also to our service for the Saviour.

This book answers many questions about churches and church membership in New Testament times. Next to having a real walk with Christ and knowing the doctrines of the faith, membership of a good church has a powerful formative influence on the believer's life.

God's Rules for Holiness
Unlocking the Ten Commandments
Peter Masters
139 pages, paperback, ISBN 978 1 870855 37 2

Taken at face value the Ten Commandments are binding on all people, and will guard the way to Heaven, so that evil will never spoil its glory and purity. But the Commandments are far greater than their surface meaning, as this book shows.

They challenge us as Christians on a still wider range of sinful deeds and attitudes. They provide positive virtues as goals. And they give immense help for staying close to the Lord in our walk and worship.

The Commandments are vital for godly living and for greater blessing, but we need to enter into the panoramic view they provide for the standards and goals for redeemed people.

For other Wakeman titles please see www.wakemantrust.org